ENGINEERED

For

GLORY

by

John T. and Ruth Seamands

with

A Tribute by David A. Seamands

Francis Asbury Society, Inc.

Francis Asbury Society, Inc.
Box 7
Wilmore, Kentucky 40390

Francis Asbury's eighteenth century vision was to "preach the Gospel in every kitchen in this country and to spread scriptural holiness over this land." It is the purpose of the Francis Asbury Society to pick up Asbury's pointed challenge in four areas of ministry: *evangelism, discipleship, missions,* and *Christian literature.*

ISBN 0-915143-01-1

TABLE OF CONTENTS

Table of Contents — Continued

PROLOGUE

Hot morning sun beat irrepressibly down on the unusually quiet Dharur railway station in Central India. A small group of dignitaries from the South India and Hyderabad Annual Conferences of the Methodist Church anxiously awaited the coming train. They were laden with garlands of colorful flowers to put around the neck of a man they dearly loved.

Bishops Elia Peter and Kariappa Samuel and the others had not seen Reverend Dr. Earl Arnett Seamands for eight years. At age ninety, he had difficulty traveling. Yet he would soon be with them again, leading the noisy procession to the Dharur Christian Jathra—the camp meeting he had started fifty-eight years earlier in November, 1923. To the 70,000 people attending the camp meeting, Earl Arnett was neither "Reverend" nor "Doctor" but "Thatha"—Beloved, Honorable Grandfather.

The old steam engine strained as it chugged up a hill and rumbled through the heat. Doggedly it rounded the last curve and grumbled to a stop. Passengers filled every inch of the train. Almost as many huddled on the top, rode the footboards and hung out through the open windows as were crowded into the seats.

1

Shouts of "Jaya Krist, Yesu Masi Maharajah Ki Jai!"—
Victory to the Lord Jesus, Messiah and King (in the Kanarese
language) filled the station as 2,000 people spilled out of the
train, hoisting camping equipment and children.

In the midst of the confusion, Thatha emerged slowly, a
broad smile on his face, his white hair and fair skin contrast-
ing with the dark bodies pressing around him. Blind in one
eye, with thick glasses magnifying his sight in the other, he
could survey the scene only dimly. A pacemaker kept his
heart beating, a cane helped him walk. But his face glowed a
youthful joy as he stiffly bowed his head to receive garland
after garland around his neck, building up level with the top
of his head, until he could hardly breathe through their
fragrant blossoms.

Joyfully beating drums, banging cymbals and tamborines,
and singing Kanarese hymns, the crowd fell into rhythm for
the half-mile walk to the campsite. Thatha followed the
musicians, his once long, strong stride now bent into a careful
step. Behind him pressed the crowd of women with little
children on their hips, and men balancing bundles of equipment on their heads. Scores of festooned bullock carts
carrying more families, squeaked their way through the dust.
Horns of the bullocks had been painted a brilliant red for this
auspicious occasion. This colorful procession, looking somewhat like the Children of Israel crossing the River Jordan,
crossed the small stream at the side of the camp. As they
neared the tents, louder and more frequent became the shouts
of joy—"Jaya Krist! Paramananda!"

At campsite, the air was vibrant with anticipation. New
arrivals and THATHA had come! Women squatting beside
their fires as they cooked the noonday rice and chappatties
(flat bread), quickly grabbed their babies and rushed toward
the old man. "Thatha, Thatha!" they cried. All wanted him
to touch them and to bless their children— just a touch on
the head would be enough. As the excited cry of "Thatha"
rang through the camp, the crowd became a stampede. A
large group of men formed a ring around Thatha to keep

him from being trampled. He touched as many as he could, smiling and nodding his head and saying, "God bless you." Suddenly one side of the crowd shrank back in fright. "SNAKE! Get back!" yelled camp police, raising their *latis* (clubs) to fend off a large cobra. As it slithered into a hole, one policeman grabbed its tail and began slowly pulling it out. Another quickly brought a rope and looped it several times around and around the snake, knotting it firmly, as more of its body reappeared. When the head was finally out of the hole, two men yanked the rope, swinging the cobra high in the looped rope, strangling it, as others beat it with clubs.

"Jaya Krist!"—Victory to Christ—rose the cry as the snake shuddered and writhed and finally lay still. "The cobra is dead! We shall have spiritual victory here, just as Christ Jesus was victor in bruising the head of the serpent!" someone shouted. "Jaya Krist!" roared the response.

The campers finally receded to their open fires and tents, and Thatha could survey the scene. In fifty-eight years he had seen the camp grow from a smattering of between 150 and 175 church leaders to a surging throng of 70,000. This was Thatha's home—where he belonged. He thanked God for his return to India and for all those whom he loved so dearly here. This would be a great camp meeting—people would be redeemed and challenged. As he pondered this, his mental vision faded to another camp meeting many years ago, when God challenged him in such a way it changed his whole life.

† † † †

It was August, 1912. Earl Arnett Seamands, a young engineering student at the University of Cincinnati found himself reluctantly at Camp Sychar in Mount Vernon, Ohio. He had been lured there by a Christian uncle who had invited him. Not realizing it was a Christian camp, he had accepted the invitation because he needed to borrow some money from his uncle to help pay his expenses for the coming college year.

At twenty-one years of age, he had already mapped out a

career for himself as a civil engineer, with fame and fortune as his main objectives. He was not interested in God or the church or spiritual matters—indeed he was quite rebellious against God. But under the divinely inspired preaching of the evangelists at Camp Sychar, he was already under conviction for his sins and need of a Savior.

It was Thursday, missionary day at Camp Sychar, and Arnett was seated in the rear of the tabernacle on the last bench. Bishop Lewis of China was speaking. The bishop was a good preacher and gave a comprehensive address depicting physical facts of China, describing all the building going on at that time. He was graphic about how they were constructing dams and railroads, emphasizing how more needed to be built. He appealed for helpers to go to China.

Arnett was fascinated by the address. He was thinking, *What an opportunity for an engineer!* He mentally saw himself building bridges over the Yangtse River, specializing in railway engineering with structural steel bridges. A man could make a fortune there and really become somebody!

Suddenly during the address at 10:00 a.m., while Arnett was listening to tales of China, he saw a red, fiery ribbon ablaze over the pulpit. In the light, in large silvery letters about one foot high, was spelled out a country. But it was not China. It was I—N—D—I—A! Arnett almost fell backward over the bench, he was so startled by the vision. God made it very plain to him that he was to go to India with his engineering skills. But he fought the vision, rebelling against God. He wasn't even a Christian! He'd never even been converted! So why should God tell him to go to India—his dream had just begun to be China!

Later he often said, "God had His hook into me and wouldn't let me go. Those letters of fire were the turning point of my life. It was like the Apostle Paul and his vision of the Lord; that Light struck him blind to everything else in his life."

Some may think it very foolish to consider that fiery vision as God's call to Arnett, but he was so certain that it was, that his whole life took a completely new direction. He was destined to be the first Seamands in three generations of engineers to be a different sort of engineer, and in a land other than his own. He was chosen by God—and Engineered for Glory!

1

YEARS OF PREPARATION

Arnett Seamands' parents were from two of the "First Families" of West Virginia. His mother was the beautiful former Jennie Capehart, of radiant religious Presbyterian stock from St. Albans. His father, John L. Seamands, was a nominal Methodist from Milton. The young couple moved west to Lexington, Kentucky, with their first son, Roy. And on October 5, 1891, Earl Arnett was born—on High Street in the shadow of the now First United Methodist Church. He was fond of saying, "The 'resident angel' of that church flew near, leaned over the cradle and announced to the little Presbyterian baby, 'Laddie! You are predestined to become a Methodist missionary!' "

Arnett came from a family of railroad men. His grandfather served as a conductor on the Chesapeake and Ohio line, and three of his uncles were employed as conductors on the Missouri Pacific Line. Arnett's father, John L., started as an errand boy on the C. and O. line at the age of fifteen, later became a brakeman, and then at the age of twenty-four was promoted to the position of conductor.

Boyhood Days in Tucson

When Arnett was four-and-a-half years old, his father moved the family to Tucson, Arizona, to become a conductor on the Southern Pacific Railroad.

Once while on duty as a conductor on the Golden State Limited Express between Tucson and Yuma, John L. was shot by an allegedly insane man. John had to be relieved from duty for eleven months until he fully recovered.

He served the Southern Pacific Company for thirty-four years and retired on March 31, 1938, at the age of seventy. Meanwhile, two of his sons, Roy and Lawrence (born in Tucson) had joined the S.P.C. as engineer and brakeman respectively. John L.'s final run was dubbed "The Seamands' Express" as recorded by the *Arizona Daily Star* on that date:

> The Mexican Express will leave the Southern Pacific Station this morning at 10:40 o'clock for Nogales, Engineer Roy C. Seamands pulling the train and Lawrence C. Seamands will serve as train brakeman. Both are sons of the conductor, John L. Seamands, and in service on the Tucson Division.

Coming from a family of railroad men, one would imagine that Earl Arnett Seamands would follow in their train. But God had other plans for him in the days ahead.

When the Seamands family moved west in April, 1896, Tucson had a population of 5,731 and was, in Arnett's own words, "A rough and tough, wild and wooly frontier town." Of the three brothers, Arnett seemed to be the wild one of the family. He reveled in the exploits of the Apache chiefs Cochise and Geronimo. The Juvenile roughneck gang of those days was called "The Arizona Kids." Arnett was a fringe member and that didn't do him any good. All his later life he felt that his mother's prayers were like a fortress around him, safeguarding him through those days. She prayed for him and with him and nurtured him in the way she wanted him to go, though at the time he didn't appreciate it. He hated the week-end routine! Every Saturday afternoon the children had to take a bath. Then on Sunday morning, on went the clean clothes—long black stockings, short pants, and *shoes.* Who *ever* thought up the idea of wearing shoes in Tucson, Arizona! Bare feet were meant to be walked on! But wear them they did when they accompanied their mother to the Presbyterian church.

As a small child, Arnett's very best friend was a little Black boy. At that time in his life, color of skin made no difference to him—he and his friend loved each other. Arnett used to go often to his friend's home for meals and play. But one day his father said, "Son, people are talking about you because you go to that colored home." For the first time the sin of race prejudice reared up in his heart and he dropped his good friend. As he grew, his race prejudice also grew.

In 1903, when Arnett was eleven and one-half years old, his mother died. His rudder was gone, he was lost and didn't know what to do but drift. His father was often absent because of his job, and the boys got into several scrapes, especially Arnett. He tells about one time:

> There was a guy who bullied me unmercifully every time we met. One day an encounter occurred in front of a meat market on West Congress Street. I was very good with my slingshot and when the bully started toward me, I was ready this time. I loaded my slingshot with a small steel slug, and took aim at my enemy's forehead at a twenty-foot range. I intended to kill him and get rid of him forever. But my guardian angel jerked my aim down to his shin. The slug glanced off his shin, hit the sidewalk, ricocheted and went through the plate-glass window, striking the bookkeeper. Fortunately, he wasn't hurt much. Divine intervention saved that bully from sudden death—he ran off yelling and holding his bloody shin. I could have been a teen-aged murderer! My dad fixed it up with the sheriff and paid for a new window for the meat market.

Another time Arnett got into a fight with a Mexican boy. His opponent picked up a rock and hit Arnett in the head, cutting a big gash. The boy ran away, leaving Arnett with a bloody head and shirt. It took nine or ten stitches to close the wound.

At that time there were no electric street lights in Tucson, so Arnett got a job going around, filling and lighting lamps every night. One night he and his brother Roy were walking home down a very dark street, with only a small moon visible. As they neared a certain spot they saw a dark round shadow on the dirt road. Roy was smoking and he lit a match, holding it close to the spot. It was a big pool of blood! But something was shining here and there in the blood. They dipped their hands in and found eight silver dollars—a real fortune! Nobody used paper money in Tucson—everything was paid for in coins. The two boys took their loot home, washed off the blood, then divided the money. Four dollars each! They were so excited they couldn't keep quiet about their find and soon everyone knew about it.

A few days later the sheriff came to their house, called them out and said, "Boys, we hear you found eight dollars. Well, we're sorry, but you'll have to give the money back— it doesn't belong to you. See—one of the trainmen was coming home that night and a guy waylaid him and robbed him. He tried to fight, but the robber shot him—that's where all the blood came from. He later died and this money belongs to his widow. Now we've caught the robber."

"How'd you catch him?" Arnett asked.

"Well, you see this man got a lot of money from the train-man. What you boys found was just a few of the coins he dropped while he was making his getaway. But he has a wife who likes fancy clothes. And the last few days she's been spending money like water, so we investigated. We got him. They'll have a trial next week, and he'll probably hang."

The prediction was correct. The culprit was sentenced to die on a gallows to be erected outside the courthouse in Tucson. Arnett and Roy decided that since that thief had cost them their four silver dollars apiece, they were going to see him hang. So they went early, crawled up on the roof and had a ringside seat. When the condemned man was brought out, he was joking with his executioners. He said, "Now be sure to get that hood on me straight. Don't go messin' up this job!" Arnett and Roy watched, but when the trap was sprung, Arnett blinked. He couldn't quite manage to watch that part. He said he thought that was the last hanging inside the city of Tucson. Those later condemned were taken outside the town and hanged on a tree.

When it was decided in Tucson that a high school was needed, the question arose, where to put it? A city ordinance directed that a school could not be built close to a saloon—but saloons were numerous. So the first high school building was an old adobe on the edge of the city in challa cactus and rattlesnake country. Arnett was one of the 45 charter students at the first high school of Tucson, Arizona, started in 1906. Problems in the school of that day were not the problems of today. There were no drugs, no cigarettes, and no drinking. In fact, the girls had a motto: "The lips that touch wine shall never touch mine!"

At first there were no balls or bats or hoops for the students to play with, so they made their own bats with tree limbs, using tin cans for bases. The second year the school was moved into town where there was a playground. In its third and fourth years, a new building with a gym was erected, so football, baseball, and basketball teams were organized. Arnett loved baseball and he was pitcher of the team "The Tucson Greys." He was an excellent player and runner; long and lanky, he could also pole-vault eight feet. He developed great physical stamina—with his athletics and long hikes—and a ruggedness which would be invaluable for him in years to come.

Arnett's initial confrontation with God's plan for his life came during his first year of high school. He tells it this way:

One Sunday morning I was walking to a little Presbyterian church. God, through His Holy Spirit spoke ever so clearly to my young mind: "Son! Give me thine heart! Be a Christian."

But before walking the next block I rejected and settled that issue. Looking across Tucson's unbuilt open areas of those days I saw many of my young Methodist pals entering the red brick Methodist church. I quickly reasoned, or un-reasoned, that a real Christian would have to leave off all worldly pleasures and there would remain no joys in life. A Christian would have to be only a goody-goody person, a kind of sissy. I settled the matter then by saying, "When I get old and about ready to die, I'll join the church and be good!" I maligned those Methodists, not knowing that in a few years I would be a joyful, hilarious one myself!

He loved to hike and camp and many times made eighty-five miles during a weekend. He and some of his friends would finish their lessons on Wednesday nights, make good preparations for four days, and then at 1:00 a.m. start off to the Catalina mountains, thirty-two miles ahead. Arnett would lead the pack, go twenty miles with his long strides (he was six feet, one and one-half inch tall), then lie down and sleep until the rest caught up with him. Then on up into Mt. Lemon—10,000 feet. There they would camp for two days at Weber Camp. Early Sunday morning it was back to Tucson—down trail for fourteen miles to Sabino Canyon, then eighteen miles into Tucson via Ft. Lowell, and be in Tucson by supper time.

They also had long bicycle escapades. His three-hour, eighteen-minute record from the crotch up between Old and Little Baldy in the Santa Ritas, and back into Tucson on old-time sandy wagon roads, still stands. It was a distance of fifty-five miles.

During his high school summers, the Southern Pacific Railroad started to build a branch south to Nogales—sixty-five miles. Arnett got a job helping to build the tracks. Because of extreme heat in the daytime—114° in the shade—they often worked at night. The men slept in box cars and transferred from place to place on a two-handle pump car. Six men could ride on it at one time. Once Arnett was pumping the handle with his back to the direction in which they were going. Suddenly the men yelled, "Look out!" Arnett turned just in time to see a big steer on the track, but they couldn't stop. The car hit the steer, killing it instantly, and Arnett flew right between the horns and landed clear at the other end. No one was hurt in the melee.

Once their sleeping box car was parked at a railroad rock quarry on the Benson-Nogales branch. A handsome gentleman wearing a Stetson hat, a 3-piece suit—obviously a Somebody—walked up and said to the big group of workmen: "Come on, boys, let's go fishin'. That hole down there in the quarry is 15 feet deep and full of trout. Now go back to that caboose and bring some gunny bags!"

The workers looked at one another and said, "We ain't got no poles—how can we go fishin'?"

The nattily dressed gentleman pulled out a stick of dynamite. "With this!"

They shook their heads. "No! No! We'll all land in jail if we use dynamite!"

"No fear, boys," the man answered, and pulling back the lapel of his coat exhibited a big shiny star on his vest which announced, "SHERIFF OF TOMBSTONE."

Well, if the Sheriff of Tombstone wanted to use dynamite to fish, who would arrest him? So all the railroad workers, including many Americans, Indians, and people living nearby, came running with gunny bags, baskets, tubs—anything which would hold fish. One man even took off his sombrero. The first stick of dynamite fizzled out and nothing happened. The sheriff lit another one and tossed it down into the water. BANG! Immediately the top of the water was covered with dead trout, lying bellies up. Everyone scrambled down the rocks to collect fish. They had all they wanted to eat, and even took fish into the nearby town and distributed them to people on street after street! Fishing with dynamite! Arnett said, "I later realized that the Gospel of Jesus Christ is the dynamite which made me a fisher of men! That sheriff taught me a great lesson."

Arnett had decided that he wanted to be a mining engineer

and he could study at the university in Tucson. There were many mines—such as copper—in Arizona and he could see himself successful in this field. But divine intervention changed his mind. His high school math teacher, Julia Atkinson, gave him an article she thought he might like to read. There it was! A description of the newly inaugurated "Co-op" technique of engineering education by the University of Cincinnati. The plan had begun in 1906. It consisted of an in-school program for two weeks and then an at-work experience for two weeks, rotating all through five years of university training. Theory and practice; earning and learning. It was ideal for one like Arnett who would have to work his way through. His decision was immediate. Goodbye University of Arizona just six blocks away. He was bound for Cincinnati, 2,000 miles east. And little did he realize it, but on another 9,000 miles was India!

He was graduated from Tucson High School in 1910; there were ten graduates. He decided to work for a year before going to Cincinnati, intending to save all he could for college costs ahead. So he worked as timekeeper on an engineering job thirty miles south of Yuma, Arizona, on the Mexican border.

The great Colorado River had ceased to flow into the ocean and was running wild down an irrigation ditch back into southern California, forming the present Salton Sea. The United States Government and Southern Pacific engineers were trying desperately to bring the mighty Colorado back into her natural bed to flow into the Gulf of California.

On this job, for the first time he encountered real Indians from India; he had known only American Indians before. He was already loaded with race prejudice. There they were—Indian "coolies" helping to cut a right-of-way through the Mexican jungle for a safety-levee on the west bank of the Colorado. At that time Mexico admitted such coolie labor, but U.S.A. would not.

He saw the real Indians in their peculiar native dress. He heard their strange language, saw their dark faces with their *jutus* (long tufts of hair indicating Hinduism), their *butus* (red caste marks) on their foreheads. He smelled their hot curry, laughed at their foreign mannerisms, belittled their musical lyrics, and crude instruments, and ridiculed their idolatrous worship of many gods. His old, carnal race prejudice got the ascendency in his unsaved heart. He thoroughly despised them—in fact he had a vehement hatred for them.

Years later in commenting on this experience he said:

> I committed a mammoth blunder when I went east laughing about those Indians and reporting that"Indians are the scum of the earth!" I didn't at that time know Christ and His love for all people, so I made such a stupid decision. Shame on me! But I am sure my sinful thoughts precipitated action in Heaven. He who is pure Love must have overheard the thoughts of my heart and then God said to Himself, "I'll really fix this fellow! I'll give him such a love for the Indian people that it will go with him to his dying day! He will want to serve them all his life." Shame on me for harboring such thoughts about such wonderful folk. But long ago I found forgiveness, and have spent a lifetime making abundant restitution."

College Days in Cincinnati

In July, 1911, Arnett's father gave him a round-trip railway pass to Cincinnati. "Arnett, if you don't like it by Christmas, you can come back," he said.

So Arnett started eastward, never dreaming that he would be traveling eastward for the rest of his life—as far as one can go.

Arriving in Cincinnati, he met the author of the co-op plan, Dean Herman Schneider, a tremendous character. Dean Schneider sent four of the new students, including Arnett, to Mattoon, Illinois, to work on the local section gang of the Big four Railway, ten hours a day, at 16½ cents per hour! Excellent room and board cost $5 per week. Their foreman was tough, but they stuck it out until college opened in September. When school opened, they alternated every two weeks—two weeks in college, and two weeks on the job. In the fall they were transferred up to Cleveland for section work in the Lynndale yards of the Big Four. They got a raise to 17½ cents per hour. Room and board was still $5 per week—the standard for years.

The co-op plan worked to Arnett's satisfaction, in fact his pride and joy at being a co-op student and graduate never ended.

On November 19, 1911, Arnett met Yvonne Emily Shields. It was during one of his two-week stints on the job in Cleveland, Ohio. At that time he was working on a bridge. Yvonne was a beautiful girl who had a lyric soprano voice and was, at that time, studying music with an eye to grand opera. But God can use voices trained for grand opera to glorify Him in India or anywhere else, and over the years the spirits of many missionaries and Indians have been renewed listening to her beautiful singing. But of course she had no inkling of that when she met Arnett. She had been raised in a wealthy, cultured home, and this red-haired Arnett Seamands intending to become an engineer would no doubt become wealthy, too. He was socially acceptable to her family.

The romance began to flourish. They saw each other often on Arnett's two-week trips to Cleveland from Cincinnati. Arnett says, "We courted each other for three years, mostly by remote control." Yvonne was very happy with her engineer and they planned for a fine life together.

But change was coming! Arnett writes in his memoirs:

In the first year of my course in Cincinnati the plot thickened. My mother's brother, John Capehart, was a traveling businessman. He was a sterling Christian gentleman—a Spirit-filled and sanctified soul-winning witness for Christ. He had long prayed for me out in "wicked" Arizona. Now Mother's prayers were to touch me in the person of her own brother.

One day Uncle John visited me at my boarding house in Clifton, in Cincinnati. We were alone in the room. God had me cornered this time! Immediately after personal greetings, Uncle John was used of God to send the arrow straight home to my young, wayward heart. "Arnett! Are you a Christian?"

My dazed look as he saw me try to parry off the pointed question brought on the second shot. He described plainly how wonderful a Savior Christ was, how His precious shed blood would cleanse me from all sin, and how blessed a life could be mine if only I surrendered to Him!

The supper bell saved me from this confrontation, and I was relieved when Uncle John departed. John left but God didn't! The lad who started on "vacation" in early August, 1912, was by then a hard case for God to handle. Engineering ambitions now fairly consumed me. I would build the world's biggest bridge and incidently make big money and be a big shot! I had rejected God's overtures and was almost hell-bent in love with the world and the sins of my youth!

One day I received a postcard from Uncle John saying, "Arnett, I'm here at Camp Sychar, a beautiful restful place located in Mt. Vernon, Ohio, about 45 miles northeast of Columbus. You must need a little vacation by now, so come on up and spend the weekend with me."

The notation "Camp Sychar" lured me. God may not be the author of confusion, but He sure let me get confused. I pictured it as a chautauqua spot where I could have great fun. I was totally ignorant of what Camp Sychar was until Saturday afternoon, August third, when I alighted from the old-time horse-drawn streetcar in front of Camp Sychar's ancient gate. Imagine my surprise when I read the words, "Holiness Camp Meeting" written across the entrance. I gasped. Suddenly the music of hymns fell upon my ears and then I realized this was a religious camp! I turned around to retrace my steps back to work. But again stopping, I reasoned that I had spent hard-earned money for the trip, and I needed to borrow some money from Uncle John for my second year of engineering school. So I would go in and stick it out until Sunday afternoon. Gritting my teeth against God, I went on in. It cost me a dime to get in—it was to cost me my life, future talents, my all to get out!

The great ambush had begun, and God had me! The path into Sychar was to become the way into Christ's Kingdom and His service. By love God lured me to Sychar and I didn't go home on Sunday. I stayed a week and that was a kind of an OK-Corral-Spiritual Shootout. My mind was so steeled at the first against becoming a Christian, Christ literally ambushed me. My stubborn will was broken. No doubt that's what Uncle John wished for!

Three great preachers of that day occupied the pulpit at Sychar throughout the week. They were Joseph H. Smith, J.L. Brasher, and H.C. Morrison. Anyone in religious circles knows what towering giants of the pulpit these men were. How could just one engineer-in-the-making withstand those powerful preachers, filled with the Spirit of God? Arnett couldn't. He began to pray some, but did not receive any spiritual experience.

Then on Thursday, that great missionary vision of India in fiery letters on red, assaulted his senses. God wanted him in India—he knew it. But he persisted in his stubborn determination to be a great engineer for his own glory. He was rebellious that God would shock him with such an idea. *I, a missionary to India? Impossible! Unthinkable!* He remembered when he had first seen some Indians how he had despised them—and now God wanted him to go and live among them and serve them! Absolutely ridiculous!

But, on the final Sunday of the camp when Joseph H. Smith was preaching in the afternoon service, the young engineer ceased his resistance (for a time) and surrendered himself to God. The burden was suddenly lifted as he prayed at Camp Sychar's altar, and his heart was filled with peace and joy in the Lord.

But Arnett's struggle was not over. For the first two weeks after his return to Cincinnati he rejoiced in his new experience, but soon the old gang began to pull him back into his old life. Once again the lure of the world and the thrill of an engineering career began to get hold of his heart.

The vision of India was pushed into the background but still kept haunting him. "I went through the following year only half Christian," he told us.

An incident during this time, however, brought him back to his spiritual senses and once again face to face with his original call.

While at work on the railway one day, he fell backward off a flatcar, head first, onto the concrete platform of the station at Franklin, Ohio, while the section-train was moving at a speed of 20 miles per hour. His miraculous escape from death was a reminder that God had a new life in store for him and was giving him another chance to accept God's will.

In the summer of 1913, Love pulled him back to Camp Sychar. On the train between Columbus and Mt. Vernon on the Pennsylvania line, tired of the burden of guilt in his heart, and tired of rebelling against God, he finally bowed his head and said his eternal "Yes, Lord!" Simply, but with all that was within him he said, "Here, Lord, you take me and clean me up." Sweet peace and joy flooded his soul.

He told Yvonne about his call to India and his conversion. It was a great shock to Yvonne, who had pictured herself as the wife of a successful and wealthy engineer. But she loved Arnett, and her grandfather had always taught her that a wife should be willing to go wherever her husband's work takes him, and not to interfere with it at all. So, in spite of her own disappointment at the turn of destiny, and in spite of the fact that she did not feel a personal call to India, she agreed to marry Arnett and go to India with him.

Once a few years ago while talking to Mother and Dad Seamands, I (Ruth) learned that Mother had been engaged before she ever met Dad. That surprised me for I had not known about it before, even though by that time I had been in the family for thirty-five years!

"Well, Mother, had you already broken your engagement to the other man when you met Dad?" I asked.

"Yes, I had," Mother answered.

"Why did you do that? What was wrong with the man?"

"Well, he was spoiled," Mother Seamands said. "So was I! He was a mama's baby and always had everything he wanted . . . so did I! But I never pouted. When he didn't get his way with everything, he pouted. He'd get angry at me for something and would pout and not speak to me for several days. Now I had a temper too, and I got good and tired of that, so I just broke the engagement."

Dad interrupted our conversation: "Yes, she turned down a pouter and married a shouter!"

After his surrender to God on the train, Arnett stayed a week at Camp Sychar, drinking in sermons to strengthen his faith. He knew that when he got back to Cincinnati he would have to find a church home. His Uncle John suggested he go down to Wesley Chapel on East Fifth Street. Uncle John said he had heard it was a great tithing church, so it must be spiritual.

Back in Cincinnati, Arnett tried two or three churches, but did not feel at home in them. Then he checked out Wesley chapel, and he began to love that church with a love that lasted to his dying day. In his own words:

> I walked over to Wesley Chapel for church. I was headed home this time! Hallelujah! I would soon cease to be very largely working out my own salvation as a loner. I would be in the company of beautiful people of exemplary Christian life, with a unique program, imbued with the guidance of the Holy Spirit that I sorely needed.
>
> A few steps inside Wesley's large front entrance, I was no longer a loner. Four youngish men stood there ready to greet people, especially newcomers, with an unforgettable welcome of love. They were Brothers Badgley, Chipman, Gloystein, and Myers—four of the many I was to know intimately and to love fervently. That bright, bouyant welcome I will never forget!
>
> Two of them ushered the visiting young engineering student to a convenient section forward in the pews where, in God's providence, I was to worship for the next three years. Wesley's congregation was robust at that time; the folks sang lustily and

joyfully. Reverend Gervaise Roughton preached in his usual fervent style, a simple but rich Gospel message. The offering took on a somewhat strange newness to me. It was announced as "tithes and offerings." The Holy Spirit permeated the entire service, giving me the long-looked-for spiritual thrill that my young heart had been seeking. Later I met the pastor and sensed that I was in a blessed "Brotherhood." I knew I was HOME!

Wesley Chapel was to become a Missionary Training School for me. It was one of the most outstanding tithing churches of that time. For all tithers, there was no "church pledge." All signed the "tithe covenant" with one another to "bring the tithe into the storehouse." An envelope for payment was provided. There was no name on it. An act of loving obedience to Malachi 3:10 was the view of tithing.

Pastor Roughton's messages were constantly aimed in the direction of bringing people to know Jesus Christ as a personal Savior. During summer months, out-door services were held in front of the church beside the sidewalk, declaring Christ as the Wonderful Savior He is to the evening passersby and inviting them into the service.

Wesley Chapel's people were tops in giving amongst the several down-town Cincinnati Methodist churches. The church, in fact, gave more to Methodist missions than all the others combined. The "storehouse" financial plan worked beautifully.

Gervaise Roughton was a super-outstanding pastor. Famed in downtown Cincinnati all the 34 years of his pastorate of Wesley Chapel, he was a bachelor when I first met him. He moved almost night and day amongst the poor and needy, ministering in Christ's name to the sick, the dying—anybody and everybody in need of a loving touch. Saint and sinner loved him. The police force all knew him and often helped him in finding those in serious need. This beautiful spirit was a glowing example in word and deed to this budding minister and potential missionary.

Pastor Roughton was a man of prayer and divine wisdom. His sound advice helped me avoid a very unwise move I was considering in the fall of 1914—in my fourth year of engineering college. I was thinking to myself that if I were going to become a missionary, then perhaps I should cut loose from engineering college without finishing my course, and go down to Asbury College, a fine Christian school. The Holy Spirit led me to confer with my pastor. After a short period of thought, then prayer, Brother Roughton looked me square in the eyes and said, "Brother Seamands, I advise you against such a move. Asbury College is a good school. But don't have anything incomplete to your discredit! Finish your engineering course!" It was sound advice.

During the time of his association with Wesley Chapel, Arnett became a fervent witness for Christ. Trained by Brother Roughton, he began immediately to work for God in Cincinnati, witnessing to bums, harlots, down-and-outs— anyone who would talk with him. He was growing in grace.

Arnett's motives were not perfected overnight. He was converted and he'd cleaned up his life. He knew that God wanted him to go to India, but he could still see himself as "the successful engineer"—not for God, but for Arnett.

But he was daily reading his New Testament and he began to study and contemplate the work of the Holy Spirit in a Christian's life. He realized that his own motives were not all they should be. He knew that he fell short of the Christian standard found in the Apostles after they had experienced Pentecost, and his heart yearned for his own Pentecost. But he did not how to obtain it; he was full of doubtings.

For one thing he was not sure whether he was in God's will to marry Yvonne, but he loved her and did not want to give her up. Yet, he wanted the Holy Spirit in his life. So he argued with God many times about this matter. On December 24, 1913, he asked Yvonne to marry him and wrote in his diary:

"'Twas the day before Christmas! [He was visiting Yvonne's home in Cleveland during the Christmas holidays.] Did housework in the morning, wrote a few cards, then Yvonne and I had the day to ourselves in the afternoon. We had a fine talk and I finally managed to 'propose' to her and was accepted both by

Bonnie [his pet name for Yvonne] and her mother. Happiest time in my life—entering upon a new epoch! Joy!! We remained up until 10:30—talking about future. May God's blessing rest upon us and may He guide us safely through life—unto salvation in Heaven!"

All during the year of 1914 Arnett was growing in grace, but still seeking the infilling of the Holy Spirit. Though engaged, there was no possibility of marriage at that time, for financial reasons. The next Christmas vacation with Yvonne in Cleveland found him ambivalent about their plans. He wrote in his diary:

Mon. Dec. 24, 1914, we talked over the future and decided on June, 1915 as the month. *I was only half-hearted in the affair—not knowing exactly if it was God's will and feeling convicted that He didn't approve of my actions.*"

A few days later, on Jan. 2, 1915, he wrote:

Arrived in Frankfort, Kentucky for a visit with Uncle John, Jessie and Aunt Rosa. Under deep conviction now that God desired me to give up Yvonne. In a veritable *Hell* of doubt and despair! Had as good time as possible under the circumstances.
Arrived back in Cincinnati Saturday, still under terrible conviction. Could have jumped in the river! Still in Hell! . . . Missed church, missed prayer meeting on Jan. 6 for first time. Still trying to talk back to God, but it won't go!

On January 7, 1915, a snowy evening, he was walking down Clifton Avenue in front of the University of Cincinnati, his books tucked under his arm. He was talking to the Lord. "Lord, I am still hungering and thirsting for Your Spirit. I want to be cleansed by your Spirit more than anything else. I give in. I will write to Yvonne and say that it could never be God's will for us to marry!" The decision was made. His diary goes on to say:

Years of Preparation / 23

But I hadn't walked a block further when God opened the windows of Heaven and poured out such a blessing upon me that I could scarcely contain it. Glory to His precious name! And he spoke to poor wretched me as plain as day, telling me to tell her [Yvonne] to give her heart and life to God and then for me to bring her down here with me as soon as possible. Hallelujah! My sacrifice is returned. Praise Him who "will withhold no good thing from those who walk uprightly."

The whole place seemed to be bathed in divine light. His soul was baptized by the Holy Spirit and fire. God's love deluged him; it completely filled him and so overwhelmed him that he was swept with an avalanche of joy. He felt such delirious joy that he simply fell to his knees. He didn't even feel the cold, wet snow. He prayed for a long time. Then he got up, rushed over to a nearby bandstand, and for about two hours just sang and praised the Lord in sheer spiritual ecstasy. He simply could not keep quiet. His one desire was to do God's will for the rest of his life.

And now, with God's direction, he wanted to marry Yvonne. He writes:

Why not? We had been going together (courting by remote control) since November 19th, 1911, when we first met. Marrying while yet in college then was not as popular as it is now. But why not? In those "golden years" I had been faring fine with excellent room and board for $5.00 per week. And they said that two could live as cheaply as one (?)! I had a good co-op job down in the Big Four Railway office—paying $75.00 per month. That was a sound basis for this loving leap of faith! The dear Lord has proven we were right!"

He and Yvonne were married before the fireplace in Yvonne's home on February 22, 1915. He had not told any of his friends in Wesley Chapel of his marriage plans. The next Sunday when Yvonne went to church with him, one young lady rushed up and asked, "Why Arnett! Isn't she sweet! Why haven't you brought her to Wesley Chapel before? She must be your little sister, isn't she?

Arnett stood quite dumbfounded, but Yvonne, being quicker, stood up tall and announced, "No, I'm his wife!"

The lady's mouth fell open and Yvonne, with a woman's brilliant intuition, realized that the lady had, no doubt, been fancying herself married to Arnett!

Life went along well for the young couple for the next year and a half while Arnett finished his engineering education at the University of Cincinnati. They both worked in Wesley Chapel Church in their spare time, Yvonne many times singing solos. Both grew in grace and in love with each other.

In 1916, having the highest cumulative average over the period of five years in the university, Arnett graduated at the very top of his class in Civil Engineering. The top prize was a two-year paid scholarship to the University of Illinois, and an offer of a very good job with a high salary from the New York Central Railway, plus promise of a glowing future. But Arnett had experienced that other kind of glow and it had changed his whole life. So at the graduation he received his prize, then turned and gave it to the one who stood second in his class. This was Mr. Bernard Pepinsky, who for many years was a successful engineer in Cincinnati. He and Arentt remained good friends until Bernard died in 1975.

In 1982 Arnett wrote this article about his good friend, Bernard:

> During the spring of 1916 three unforgettable episodes combined to bring Bernard Pepinsky and me very close together as co-op C.E. pals. Behind us was the buildup of a five-year relationship.
>
> We had stood the test of working "on the section" together in Mattoon, Illinois, under the so-called "toughest" foreman on the Big Four Railway, Gus Pelance, during July and August, 1911, before entering the civil engineering course at the University of Cincinnati in September. Those "golden days"—10 hours

a day at 16½ cents per hour. As "alternates" we worked under the Italian section foreman, Vita Lia, in the Lyndale Yards of the Big Four in Cleveland during the terrific winter of 1911-1912. One memorable morning when we reached the job the thermometer registered 32° below zero. After proving faithful in Mattoon, we got a raise in Cleveland—17½ cents per hour!

Bernard and I had been a part of a group of a dozen co-ops who worked all summer in 1912 on the "extra gang," replacing heavier rail on the Springfield-Toledo branch of the Big Four, out of West Liberty, Ohio. Ten hours daily at 20 cents per hour. We sweated it out together, becoming closer friends all the time.

After the historic "Dayton Flood" of March, 1913, our work companionship continued on the Big Four Bridge Gang over the summer of 1914. We saw the three wrecked bridges over the Miami River north of Middletown, Ohio, restored. Bernard and I became expert spikers, often working together as a team. Still ten hours a day—but better pay—25 cents per hour!

We were companions also during the summer of 1914 as co-workers on the King Bridge Shops, St. Clair Avenue, Cleveland, helping fabricate many members of the proposed new 3-hinged and 2-level bridge on West Superior Avenue over the Cuyahoga River. Ten hours a day—25 cents per hour—oh, such fun! Bernard and I were close friends.

Since 1913 as a Christian, I increasingly endeavored to maintain a "winsome" witness by word and deed that would convince Bernard (of Russian-Jewish background)—that Christ the Messiah had truly come and wanted to be his Savior too!

The Engineering College kept Bernard and me closely linked by assigning us together on the project of designing the new roadway connecting McMillan Street and the new gym in Cincinnati, during the Spring of 1915. We also supervised its construction. I coveted him for Christ!

When the matter of a graduating thesis came up, Bernard and I requested the privilege of working together on a big joint project. This was allowed—as evidenced by a bound book by "Pepinsky and Seamands." Also by the tracings of the drawings on the project which we keep to this day—60 years after graduation!

Our minds and hearts were very close together the six months we worked on this "master-sized project!"

On a February morning the big day came. I went into our classroom and went to my desk. Bernard was there ahead of me. We smilingly greeted one another. As I was arranging my desk for the day, suddenly Bernard confronted me and excitedly said, "Arnett! We'll have to admit that God has done wonders for you!"

Ah! Here was my chance—the time was flying by so fast—we would soon graduate and go our separate ways!

"Yes, Bernard! God, my heavenly Father, through His only begotten Son, my Savior, Jesus Christ has done great things for me. He has saved me from my sins. I'm heartily sorry for my life as you saw it the first year we worked together. But Jesus Christ has made the change! He's a . . ."

Bernard interrupted, "But he hasn't come yet!"

Knowing his Jewish faith, I remained firm. "You are wrong, Bernard! The Christ HAS come—He has come into my heart!"

"No, Arnett. He hasn't come yet!"

"Yes, He has, Bernard—He's a wonderful reality in His saving power today!"

"No! He hasn't come yet!"

"Now, Bernard, I'm aware of your scientific mentality—you have to put everything in the test tube and know for yourself. Let me suggest a test—the same one I went through, and you will, I'm sure, arrive at my knowledge by experience. Tonight before you retire, you just get down on your knees by your bedside and in all humility say, 'Oh, Christ! IF you have come, please come into my heart!' You will know the amazing fact of His coming. He will come into your heart just as He has come into mine and lives there the Victor today!"

"No, Arnett—he hasn't come yet!" insisted Bernard. He insisted. I insisted! But we remained fast friends, and by July we had completed our super-thesis happily together.

There was yet another event of great interest due that fateful spring of 1916 before graduation. One March morning when I arrived in our classroom, the boys were all buzzing in an excited conversation. I listened with interest as they were saying, "It is either Pepinsky or Seamands! They're figuring it out now!"

Naturally, I inquired what was going on. I was totally ignorant of the fact that there was a two-year, $800-a-year scholarship for post-graduate studies in the University of Illinois awaiting the senior in Engineering College who had the highest average of grades for the full five-year course.

Eventually the figure came out—it was Seamands! Bernard was a very close second. So Seamands turned to Pepinsky and said, "Bernard! I'm headed for India as a missionary! It's all yours!" Bernard got the scholarship, used it one year and then had to enlist for World War I. He missed the second year of his scholarship.

Across the decades—by correspondence and by personal contact on every furlough—Bernard and I remained the finest of friends. Like Arnett, Bernard never really retired. He was the head of "Pepinsky and Associates, Architects" in Cincinnati when we last had lunch together. J.T. and Ruth, David and Helen and I were in Cincinnati for the Good News Convocation during the summer of 1972. All the Seamandses and Bernard and his adorable wife, Sadie, were to have enjoyed a supper reunion. But Sadie became ill and the cherished event became impossible.

Sadie left Bernard a lonesome husband by her death in December, 1973. His married daughter, Dulcy Schottenfels, living in Cincinnati, was a great comfort and help to him. But early in 1975 Bernard himself became seriously ill—and death came on May 6, 1975. I, too, have been real lonesome for my true co-op pal ever since his passing.

With Dulcy's help, by letter and phone, I kept in close contact with Bernard while he was in the hospital. I tried to comfort my friend by word and prayer. All those days I fervently prayed unceasingly for Bernard, "Dear Lord! Please by the Holy Spirit remind Bernard of our memorable conversation in the classroom back in February 1916, and help him to believe and receive Christ as his Savior! Let him know his Messiah has come!" This was my pointed, ceaseless prayer of faith for my dear co-op pal. James 5:15 promises, "And the prayer of faith shall save the sick, and the Lord shall raise him up; and if he have committed sins, they shall be forgiven him."

Dare I believe that Bernard and I will meet again in the new Jerusalem—this time together in the employ of the Chief Engineer of the Universe—Christ, the Creator, for "All things were made by him, and without Him was not anything made that was made!" (John 1:3). Lord Jesus! I believe!

E. Arnett Seamands

First Pastorate in Pemberville

Ever since Arnett had given his heart to Christ, his thoughts had more and more been turning toward the ministry. He knew he should go to India as a Christian missionary-engineer, but realized he should also have some Bible and arts courses before going. Arnett's notes tell us:

The depth of our adoption into the great Wesley family was manifest before my graduation in June, 1916. We had the church leaders' full confidence. They offered us a proposition, fully paid up. They felt I would be a better missionary if I had the arts courses—English Bible, psychology, history and the like. They introduced me to our Ohio Northern University, Ada, Ohio, where I received full credit for all my science subjects at U.C. I earned a B.S. degree at Ada in one year by taking only the arts subjects. Wesley Chapel provided the year's tuition and gave me $800 to live on. We really belonged to Wesley Chapel!

During that year, on November 15, 1916, their first son, John Thompson, always called J.T., was born. Yvonne had gone home to Cleveland to be with her mother for the birth. The baby had red hair just like his father.

Having finished his B.S. degree, Arnett went to the West Ohio Annual Conference of the Methodist Church in 1917, which convened in Ada that year. Dr. E. E. McCammon, District Superintendent of the Toledo District, chose Arnett from among the ministerial students for appointment. He was to go to the Pemberville Circuit! He was to be a minister!

Arnett's notes give us the story:

It was a lovely mid-September afternoon, the year of our Lord, 1917, when we three arrived at the headquarters of our first preaching appointment, the oft-called Peaceful Pemberville on the Pretty Portage river. Sure, Yvonne, baby J.T. and I were real excited, as the truck with our few household articles stopped at the rear of the Pemberville Church-cum-parsonage-cum-path! We were "rarin' to go" in a love service to a people we already loved—sight unseen. When darling Mother Speck from next door came hurrying to give us a royal welcome, we knew it would be easy to love and serve our people!

Sister Speck ushered us into our new home—an integral part of the very church building. Parsonage in the rear, sanctuary in front. A door from the living room opened immediately into the sanctuary, just by the pulpit platform. Hurrah! I saw it! We could park baby J.T. in his crib right at this door and if I should not shout too loud when preaching, we could hear his cry and wife could slip in and attend to him. A wise arrangement—an early step toward the modern church nursery!

We had previously heard preachers smilingly talk of their "parsonage and PATH," and behold! we were to begin our ministry with this same blessing. It was a bit cold in winter time to walk this beaten path to the seat in the "little garage!" But we soon were used to it—after all, we were to soon find that many of our dear people had the same arrangement. So we were in good company.

Like the modern Methodist preachers, we too, in those early days, were supplied with some utilities: a fine pot-bellied hard-coal heater stove. It amazingly did the job. The heat from the living room ascended through an opening in the ceiling to warm the bedroom above and a little office adjoining. A splendid coal cooking range was already in the kitchen, with a fine hand-pump at the sink. For drinking water, the good neighbors, Specks, allowed us to share their little hand pump in the center of the yard. For bathing, our old-fashioned round zinc washtub we had brought with us.

Strangely, the full seriousness of our new venture was suddenly to break in on me the next morning. I was over in the big Hobart Bowlus store for something. Mr. Hobart, meeting me, greeted me with a big smile saying, "Welcome, REVEREND!"

Wow! "Reverend!" I never dreamed I would someday be a Reverend! The sudden sense of responsibility shocked me. "Help me, Lord!" I immediately prayed. A new era of life was before me. Indeed! Here we were in peaceful Pemberville, a three-point circuit, not knowing that actually we were three years ahead of my schedule for a Methodist missionary career in India!

And that bright vision of India which God had entrusted to him was still in his mind. It was in 1918 that Arnett met Bishop Warne, missionary bishop from India, and heard him speak. Arnett drank in every word. After the message, he went up to shake hands with the bishop and asked, "Do you need any more missionaries in India?"

Two weeks later a telegram came from the bishop, "Can you meet the missionary committee in Columbus, Ohio?"

Could he?!!

On the committee was Dr. Murray T. Titus. As a result of that meeting, Arnett and Yvonne were accepted as missionary candidates. But they finished their second year of service on the Pemberville charge, then they began to prepare for their first long term in India. In those days a "missionary term" was seven years!

2

FIRST YEARS IN INDIA

On Saturday, August 23, 1919, Arnett, Yvonne, and little J.T., almost three years old, set sail from San Francisco for India for the first time. Arnett's diary is full of comments about that long two-month trip. Following are some of them:

We are on the good ship Ecuador (Pacific Mail Steam Ship Company). As the ship slowly leaves the Golden Gate, inward tears from the separation from loved ones and of the beloved homeland teach us the poet's meaning, "Breathes there a soul so dead / Who never to himself hath said, / ' This is my own, my native land'?"

The moments of separation were strangely emotional. But the sweet burning consciousness of obeying Christ's will gave glorious victory. Hallelujah! We leave America, loved ones, and Christian comfort, that poor India may more and more have our Christ, His marvelous full salvation, and every good and perfect gift of which He is author — i.e., all our comforts, helps, and more.

. . . We had calm seas, and we had scarcely left port two hours till Yvonne was terribly seasick. Poor unfortunate girl. We helped all we could, but it was several days before she was anyways near well. I am taking complete care of the boy [J.T.].

There are about thirty missionaries aboard — mostly Baptist and Methodist — enough to be instrumental in God's hands to the salvation of many on this ship. . . . Except for one lone passing ship, we have seen only water for several days. There is plenty of high-class booze for those who are enthralled by it. . . . We are gradually getting acquainted with others on this ship — there are both tares and wheat present. Thank God for all the wheat!

. . . A big Aloha (Farewell) supper and dance was given for those departing at Honolulu. The supper was fine, but the modern dance was vulgar indeed.

. . . A second Sunday aboard this ship with no service. What would Christ's children do without the indwelling presence of the blessed Holy Ghost to teach, feed and comfort, and lead when we are not privileged with any Gospel service. Hallelujah! He abides to keep sanctified even in mid-Pacific.

. . . Extensive gambling all over ship, in steerage rear and front, also among the "400" in first class on promenade deck. Poker, Bridge, Fan-Tan. I watched "Fan-Tan" table crowd in afternoon — much money changed hands. Many women playing; our money with "In God we trust" inscribed thereon placed to such shame. I notice about the table "fast" women meagerly clad, smelling of booze and cigarette smoke. Gambling slaves, unsaved, educated, cultured Americans; and poor, unsaved unenlightened, uneducated Chinese. To one Christian there are three ungodly Americans who can tear down by their unsavory presence in the foreign land all we may build up. The Lord help our homeland preachers to get all the tourists saved before they are granted passports! (Uncle Sam might incorporate Salvation as one other requirement for the issuance of passports!)

Sunday, October 5, 1919 — my 28th birthday. Hooray! We are in Haiphong, the most beautiful harbor in the world — a fine place to spend a birthday.

On Sunday, October 26, we arrived in Colombo . . . here for two days. We must transship into a small steamer for India. Once aboard we were off toward the mainland. About an hour-and-a-half ride over to Dhanishkodi, India. Customs officials looked over all our goods and passed all without reserve. How

the little craft did rock and toss in the rough seas of the narrows.
Yvonne and others got awfully sick and if the journey had been
fifteen minutes longer I would have been likewise. At Dhanishkodi we transferred to the waiting train and with but few pre-
liminaries we were soon off for Madras.

Wednesday, October 29, we finally arrived at Kolar Town
[first assignment in India]. What joy we felt to get off at our
last station of the journey. Thanks be to our God who hath
brought us safely through! Memorable day! Memorable time as
we marched between two lines of boys and girls of Kolar schools,
who stood at attention to welcome us, into the mission compound! Our hearts were melted at the bounteous welcome and
the long, tiresome journey was quite repaid! We took a much-
needed rest for some few days.

. . . Bishop J. E. Robinson came out from Bangalore to see us.
Sweet acquaintance!

Because of Arnett's engineering training, he was labeled
by the Methodist Board as a "technical missionary," and so
was appointed as principal of the Industrial School in Kolar.
This was a school established by the mission to train Christian young men in the skills of carpentry, cabinetmaking,
ironwork, and motor mechanics. But everyone around noted
Arnett's zeal for evangelism. The bishop and cabinet members said to each other, "This young fellow is too evangelistic
to be stuck in an industrial school all his life. Let's push him
out into evangelism."

He had been in Kolar only a month when the bishop decided that Arnett and Yvonne should move into Bangalore
where they could hire a good language teacher. Learning the
Kanarese language was a "must" for anyone who was to be
an evangelistic missionary in the South India Conference of
the Methodist Church. So both of them buckled down to
language study in earnest, and gradually sounds became
words and words took on meaning.

Bangalore was probably the easiest place to live of all their
missionary career. Its climate is mild and there are beautiful

flowers and trees, with plenty of meat and vegetables and fruits. At that time it was a big British army station, so the Seamands family had the fellowship of many westerners while they were getting acquainted with India.

They had been in the beautiful "garden city" of Bangalore only a short time when Arnett was asked to be a temporary Sunday school superintendent for the Richmond Town Methodist Church. "Richmond Town" is one section of Bangalore. Near the church is Baldwin Girls School and Baldwin Boys School.

On May 25, 1920, along with his language study and Sunday school superintendency, Bishop Robinson appointed Arnett as the headmaster of Baldwin Boys High School. And at the same time the bishop appointed him as pastor of the Richmond Town Methodist Church! This was, and still is, an English-speaking church with the majority of its members from the Anglo-Indian population of Bangalore. At that time many English people attended the church, also a few Indians. It is the official church for the two high schools—students march in a body to the services. This was Arnett's new three-point charge—and each section of the appointment was a full-time job!

Arnett's first preaching service in his new church took place on Sunday, June 20, 1920. He writes in his diary:

> Just one year ago exactly since I preached my last message on the Pemberville, Ohio circuit. Here, exactly a year to the Sunday, I begin anew in this great land. Lord Jesus! Help us to live our first message to this people!

Six months later, on December 19, 1920, Arnett was ordained as both Deacon and Elder under the "Missionary Rule." Bishop H. Lester Smith performed the ceremony which took place at the South India Annual Conference session, held at Vikarabad. The conference Journal records:

> Brother and Sister Seamands have been doing valiant service

in several capacities. His fine work in Baldwin School has borne good fruit. With all the added responsibilities he managed to pass the First Year Kanarese Examination creditably. We are grateful for such promising recruits.

A few lines from Arnett's report in the same Journal:

> It has been a delight to preach to the congregation of this church. . . . Our delight in preaching, however, has especially been in the privilege of declaring the Gospel of full and free salvation for both this life and the life to come. We have endeavored to maintain the old-time evangelistic spirit in each service and we praise God that He has sent seekers to the altar. Many have become happy finders. We have founded unit-group prayer meetings . . . and [they] have been crowned with success. Stewardship sermons have been preached and thirty tithers have signed with more to follow. . . .

Arnett and Yvonne spent another year in Bangalore, studying language all the time. A notation in the Conference Journal of 1921 precipitated prayers of anguish for one area of Methodism:

> All through the circuits about Bidar the wells are dry, the crops were failures, and famine and thirst claimed both man and beast. Whole villages moved away in search of water, leaving behind their flocks and herds that could not follow. Along the highways the hungry multitudes made travel heart-breaking. Little heart had our villagers to listen to the Christian Gospel when hunger gnawed at their empty stomachs.

At the end of that conference when the appointments were read, Arnett and Yvonne were appointed to Bidar.

Bidar

The first Christian in the Bidar area had been a Hindu *sadhu* (priest) named S. Jothappa. He worshipped especially the Hindu deity *Vitoba*. In the year 1896, a new missionary by the name of Rev. Albert E. Cook came to Bidar. He stayed in a rented house in the town and many times visited nearby villages on foot, and farther villages on horseback. Sadhu Jothappa became acquainted with Rev. Cook, who witnessed to him about Christ. He told the Sadhu, "Christ is the Savior, the true God. He forgives sins and he died for sinners. No other god can save mankind."

Jothappa and his sadhu friend, Parbhappa, were much interested in this new God who could forgive sins. After some time they were convicted of their sins and convinced of the truth. They asked Rev. Cook to baptize them.

Both were baptized and immediately met hostility and persecution by their relatives and friends. They were treated as outcastes for changing their religion. Even Jothappa's own sister was forbidden to visit him. She was grieved to "lose" her brother, but after a few years she, too, believed and was baptized as the first woman to become a Christian in that area. Village farmers persecuted them by not hiring them to work, but they survived with the missionary's help.

Wherever Jothappa went he witnessed for Christ boldly in the midst of Hindus, Muslims, and others, and told them Christ only was the Savior. Some of his friends gradually accepted Christ.

The year before Arnett and Yvonne Seamands were sent to Bidar, a very great plague epidemic broke out. All the school boys and training school people moved out to camp on the mission hill. Plague is spread by fleas and rats. When plague hits a village, people all leave to set up temporary shelter elsewhere. In this plague epidemic a young school boy, related to Jothappa, became ill. There was no one who could look after the boy except Jothappa, and he nursed him for eight days before the boy died. As Jothappa left to go to his home he admonished the people to continuously sing and praise the Lord with *bhajanas* (song-fests). He told them, "Keep on worshipping the true God!" A few days later, he, too, died of plague. He had given his life for one of the little ones. He left a great Christian legacy in his five children, twenty grandchildren, and sixty-three great grandchildren!

As a young Hindu Sadhu, before Jothappa ever met Rev. Cook, he had begun to dig a cave in which to worship his Vitoba god. Everyday he went out to the hill and dug a little there. But then he was converted, and used the cave for worshipping Christ and singing Christian songs. He and his friends used to gather there every evening to praise God. In 1916 the cave was finished and was dedicated by Jothappa's son, J. Jacob, as the Christians' prayer cave. More about this cave later.

In January, 1922, Yvonne and Arnett arrived in the rugged area of Bidar. Bidar—that historic old town with its walled fort. There is a story about the building of that fort: While it was being built (before Columbus discovered America), one part of the wall kept falling down. No one could understand why. When the puzzle was taken to the Hindu priest, he said, "If you take a young girl, pregnant with her first child, and build her alive into the wall, it will stand."

At that time human sacrifice was not unknown to Hinduism, so the priest's directive was carried out. A young girl, fourteen years of age and pregnant with her first child, was built alive into the wall. As the priest promised—the wall stood and is still standing even today.

Arnett was appointed to be the new superintendent of Bidar district which is in Hyderabad State. In 1922, Bidar was still a very backward rural center, without electricity or city water supply. It was eighty miles from the nearest railway station and bakery. Tigers often prowled the mission compound at night, and at times made off with the mail-carrier who brought the mail on foot from the nearest postal center! For fresh meat, Arnett had to go out into the countryside and hunt down wild pigs and deer. It took them days to get a basket of vegetables from any city. Their small son, J.T., soon became ill with a digestive parasite which could not be cured for several years, and which almost killed him.

Their second son, David, was born in a small mission

hospital in Vikarabad, on February 6, 1922. For several days a tiger had been prowling the area, but no one had been lucky enough to shoot it. Just beyond Yvonne's hospital room window, a goat was tied up as tiger bait, and as her labor came on she could hear the goat bleating pitifully. It was easy to think she could also hear the tiger growling and ready to spring.

No—Arnett had not promised Yvonne a rose garden, and her life was not one. No doubt it had been very difficult for her to leave a fine home in the United States and end up living in Bidar under such circumstances. But she had a husband who loved her completely, and a job to do in God's kingdom. What else could any woman ask?

Anyway, she made her own rose garden—everywhere they were stationed. On every mission compound where she lived she made barren desert places bloom, interspersed with papayya, guava, and mango trees. The home she supervised was a haven for Arnett after his frequent and wearying, dusty trips to villages—preaching, building, and living the Gospel of Jesus Christ. She kept a perfect house and went to great lengths to acquire fresh fruits and vegetables and to make tempting desserts for Arnett's "sweet tooth."

Yvonne never talked about her own religious beliefs and she never testified or prayed in public. But she loved her husband and worked along with him in his every appointment.

Yvonne's father had died, and when David was born, her mother, Mrs. Ida E. Shields, came out to live with them in Bidar. She was a great comfort to Yvonne. Mrs. Shields was of Pennsylvania Dutch background, a large, rugged woman, who took tigers and cobras in her stride.

Arnett's early life in Tucson had prepared him for such a place as Bidar. To go from the arid desert in Arizona to the arid section of Hyderabad State in India was no hardship. He loved hiking. He had been used to walking miles over the mountains of Arizona with a pack on his back. He remarks on the similarities in his diary:

I was used to sleeping outdoors with mosquitoes, rattlesnakes, gila monsters, bobcats, mountain lions, horned toads, scorpions, and centipedes. This roughing it was all a preparation for touring days in India—camping out amongst tigers, panthers, pythons, cobras, kraits, scorpions and centipedes. As to food, the transition from Mexican chile con carne to India's hot curry and rice was to become delectable and easy. I was tailor-made for that part of India and the Lord knew it very well. He was planning the eventual use of all aspects of my youthful experience.

No, there was no great change in climate. The change was in the climate of Arnett's heart—from hatred to love for the Indians. God had put within him such a love for the Indian people that it was his constant rejoicing. He exhibited utmost patience and understanding. After remembering the fiery temper of his youth, this was a source of surprise to himself.

One of the outstanding contributions that Arnett made during his term in Bidar was in the area of the socio-economic life of the Christian community. He encouraged the inauguration of vocational training. Some excerpts from his Conference Journal reports mention this new dimension:

A shop for the manufacture of the celebrated Bidar-ware has been started in connection with the school, and several boys are doing very good work. It is hoped that a carpenter shop can be installed in the New Year. The beginning of a small farm has been made in connection with the school. All of this new enterprise is looking forward to a thrifty, self-supporting Christian community. Three boys are also learning tailoring.

† † † †

In January it was found possible to install a small carpenter shop. Tukaram, a Bidar boy returned from the Industrial School in Kolar, and has been the schoolmaster and has done very creditable work. This shop has its home in the bull-stalls alongside the Bidar-ware shop, but we trust that someday both these shops will have more suitable quarters and equipment.

Two of another type of village worker [instead of mission-paid] have been sent out this past year. One boy, maker of the famous Bidar-ware will now continue to make his wares out in a village under appointment from District Conference, and will preach the Gospel and care for his flock mornings and evenings. During the day he will do an honest day's work to pay two-thirds of his own expenses and show an example to his flock in the matter of "hand work."

Another, a carpenter lad, will pastor a flock under similar appointment. Of course, these boys have capable wives, the products of our own girls boarding schools. Our aim is to thus thrust out a flood of carpenters, weavers, blacksmiths, and other Christian artisans who will be both pastors and artisans, a stepping-stone to self-support in India and an invaluable band in the Christian conquest of this region.

Today Bidar is known for its Christian artisans of many types: weavers, tailors, Bidar-ware experts, blacksmiths, carpenters, stone masons, and bricklayers. By reputation these are the best for a radius of fifty miles. This is the reason for the advanced social standing of the Christians in that area. In his 1922 report Arnett mentions a great area of need:

. . . and now the good news has come that an American doctor will be in Bidar the beginning of the new year. All Bidar is happy, rejoicing, praising God *magna cum voce!* The prospect for reopening the hospital here in Bidar is indeed gladdening when one understands the terrible need for expert medical help in this great area involving 1,500,000 souls who continually cry, "Come over and help us!"

Arnett's 1923 report elaborates:

Last fall Dr. and Mrs. C.E. Pinckney arrived in our midst. The people of Bidar and environs are greatly rejoicing over . . . having expert medical help within reach. Besides the work in the station hospital, Dr. Pinckney has toured out into the district;

there he has ministered to the needs of many. Thus the medical work is a sure form of peace bond between the Mission and the Community. It is a great friend-maker and a friend-keeper.

. . . But the death roll has been practically doubled that of the previous year. This is to be accounted for in the series of epidemics which spread through the area this past year, and even now are raging. Some cholera, much influenza, then heavy onslaughts of relapsing fever and plague have brought to the grave thousands of people. Town after town has had to be evacuated completely on account of plague. Imagine a town of 6,000 people totally deserted except by hordes of rats which carry the death sting. Such is Chidguppa, one of the large towns of the Hominabad Circuit. When the doctor and I passed through we saw but an occasional straggler within the town, while the whole population had moved outside, built shelters, established new bazaars, and dug wells. And there they were abiding the time when they might freely return to their real homes.

It was in Bidar that Arnett got his start as an evangelistic missionary in the South India Conference. During this term of service, he and his colleague, Rev. M.D. Ross, conducted their first "until meeting" at *Bondla Bhavi* ("the travelers' well") and witnessed the beginning of a great Spirit-led revival movement that continued to sweep through the entire work of the Conference for the next few years. This was the revival that gave birth to the camp meeting or "Christian Jathra" movement throughout Indian Methodism.

For the next eighteen years Seamands the engineer was pushed into the background, and Seamands the evangelist came to the front. Slide rule and blueprint gave way to Bible and pulpit. Constructing buildings gave way to building character.

But, after all, is this not the divine order of Christian missions? First comes evangelism—proclaiming the Good News of Jesus Christ, to the end that men may be thoroughly converted and transformed by the grace of God and that the Church of Christ may be established. Then out of the invisible

Church comes the visible church with all of its organization
and institutions, its schools and hospitals, its agricultural and
social work, as a practical demonstration of the Gospel and
as the means by which the whole Gospel may minister to
the whole man.

This divine order proved to be God's plan for Methodism
in South India. First came evangelism. On the initiative of
the Holy Spirit, a group movement developed within the
borders of the former Hyderabad State. Dharur Jathra and
the revival that followed gave spiritual impetus and leadership to the movement. Though Indian preachers and foreign
missionaries gave direction and guidance to the movement,
the major evangelistic thrust came in the form of a powerful
lay-witness movement. Thousands were converted and
baptized, and scores of Christian congregations were organized in the villages.

Then arose the need for many new primary and secondary
schools to train leadership for the church and to afford a
basic education for the Christian community as a whole.
Need also arose for additional hospitals and dispensaries
to provide healthy bodies as a fit habitation for the Holy
Spirit. Agricultural and industrial schools were opened to
help meet basic material and economic needs. At the end
of his first conference year in Bidar, Arnett wrote in his
report:

. . . We have more than our hands full. . . . Bidar district's di-
mensions are: north to south, 50 miles; west to east, 75 miles. In
this 3,750 square miles of Deccan land are 909 towns and villages,
wholly the responsibility of Methodism. This year the crops
were good, and conditions of health fairly good. . . . The Gospel
has been preached in the power of the Holy Spirit to numbers. In
two months' time three Hindu sadhus were baptized, and another
requested baptism. . . . In one of our summer training schools
[for mission workers] the power of the Lord was especially
manifest. While the workers were being taught, crowds came
from all around and workers had to be sent out from class in

relays to preach to them from early morning until midnight. The Word of the Lord was glorified in that village and in many surrounding ones; over a hundred were baptized; many villages are now beseeching us, so that much fruit is yet to come. And the end is not yet, praise the Lord! Conviction for sin rested upon people and the enemy became angry. Non-believers stoned the camp and tried to run the workers out of town, but the Lord gave victory. After all, preaching Jesus Christ crucified does bring either Riot or a Revival — and sometimes a combination of both.

Stones to Garlands

The "stone-throwing," which Arnett mentioned in his 1921 Journal Report as a very small incident, proved to have far-reaching consequences.

Miss Rudell Montgomery, lady missionary of the Bidar District, was conducting a special training school for some village pastors and their wives in the strategic village of Kamtan, about eight miles out of Bidar. Approximately a dozen Indian couples had gathered for lectures and messages.

Kamtan had been chosen for this training school because shortly before that about a hundred-and-fifty outcaste Hindus of the village had received Christian baptism and been taken into the church fellowship. Bidar missionaries felt this training school would benefit not only village workers, but new Christians as well. Arnett was one of the instructors and preachers. A large tent was pitched in the *keri* (outcaste section of the village) in order to conduct meetings in the shade.

The occasion turned out to be much more than just a series of lectures. A real spiritual hunger led workers to give themselves to prayer and heart-searching. As a result, the power of the Holy Spirit was released in their midst and revival followed. Unbelievers in the village heard and saw what was taking place and, out of curiosity, started coming to witness the scenes of revival. Soon a steady stream of inquirers was coming and going at campsite. The workers set up a relay of preachers who proclaimed the good news of Christ from morning till night to these interested ones.

After several days Arnett had to return to headquarters at Bidar for some urgent business. Next morning at dawn he was awakened by a runner from Kamtan with news that a tense situation had suddenly developed in the village right after his departure.

That evening about a dozen Muslim residents of the village, under the leadership of a man named Ismael, had suddenly arrived at the site of the training school, armed with clubs and swords. Addressing Miss Montgomery, the American missionary, Ismael said in a loud voice, "As long as you Christians remain in this village we have no peace. You must leave immediately!"

Very calmly, yet boldly, Miss Montgomery answered, "Why do you want us to leave? On what authority do you give this order?"

"Never mind," insisted the Muslim leader, "you must leave—immediately!"

By this time the women and children, in fear, had taken refuge in the large tent where the meetings were being held. Men gathered around their missionary to defend her and also their wives. One of the village preachers was a well-built, muscular individual who looked like a prizefighter. Though unarmed, he clenched his fists and took a step or two forward, ready to meet the challenge facing his group.

Miss Montgomery took in the situation at a glance. On one side she saw the Muslim attackers with their weapons; hatred in their faces. On the other side she saw the little band of preachers, unarmed, but courageous and determined. There was fire in their eyes. The tiniest spark would ignite a bloody struggle. But her main concern was for the Master's name which was at stake.

She stepped in front of her band of workers and spoke one brief sentence: "Remember, brethren, you belong to Christ."

Her voice was like magic. The Christians dropped their hands to their sides, bent their heads in submission and said to their persecutors, "Friends, we are at your mercy. Do what you will."

The Muslims attacked. They refrained from using their swords, but they employed their clubs freely. Blow after blow rained down upon the heads and arms of the preachers. Then the Muslims rushed toward the tent and pulled up all the stakes, bringing the canvas down upon the screaming band of women and children. Meanwhile a reserve group of attackers began a shower of stones from the rear.

When Arnett received the news he rushed out to Kamtan as fast as his Model-T Ford would go. He counted one hundred and one stones at the scene. He gathered the Christian workers and congregation together, read to them out of the Beatitudes, and tried to bring them comfort and hope.

However, for future protection of the Christians, he felt it was best to report the matter to the police and ask them to prevent a recurrence of the incident. Though most of the assailants were Muslims, the Muslim police took a serious view of the matter. They threatened them with punishment if they should repeat their lawlessness, and took a written promise from Ismael and his men that they would live peacefully with their Christian neighbors in the days to come. The incident was thus considered closed.

But stones do not fall on the heads of God's children without His notice. He is able to make the wrath of men to bring praise to His name.

Twenty-four years later, in 1946, the Rev. David Seamands returned to India as a missionary and, like his father before him, was appointed superintendent of Bidar District. By this time, additional baptisms had brought the Christian membership of the Kamtan Church to between four and five hundred. Plans were afoot to construct a new church building for their growing congregation.

The following year British rule came to an end in India and the nation received her independence. The so-called "Native States"—ruled over by Indian rajahs—were given the privilege of remaining independent or joining either the Indian

Union or the new state of Pakistan. Since most of the states were governed by Hindu rajahs and the majority of their citizens were Hindus by religion, they voted to become an integral part of the Indian Republic.

The state of Hyderabad, however, presented a unique problem. The ruler was the Nizam, a Muslim ruler, while eighty percent of the citizens were Hindus. The Nizam himself was inclined to join the Indian Union, since his state was surrounded by Indian territory and Pakistan was far away. But many of his Muslim citizens objected to this move. They began to take the law into their own hands and to wreak their fury upon their Hindu neighbors. As the situation worsened, resulting in death to many people of both religions, the Indian Union finally sent troops into the area. In a four-day "police action" they took over the state, deposing the Nizam.

Then all hell broke loose. The Hindus, feeling their new power, suddenly turned upon their former Muslim oppressors, seeking revenge. For many days blood ran like water in Hyderabad, and Muslims were butchered by the hundreds.

The Muslim population in the village of Kamtan came in for its share of suffering. Many of the families fled for their lives, among them the family of Ismael who had led the attack on the small Christian group back in 1922! Ismael himself and his family, along with several relatives and friends, came to the Methodist mission compound and asked if they could find refuge there. David told them they could, but he intended to confiscate their weapons. They agreed.

The compound was already jammed with many, many Muslim families, and the storeroom was filled with all kinds of weapons already surrendered. There would be no killing on the Methodist mission compound!

David even pleaded with the new Hindu civil leaders to take special steps to prevent any new bloodshed. Within a few weeks the Central Government was able to restore law and order in the state, and the Muslim refugees were able to return to their homes. Ismael returned to Kamtan.

But it wasn't the same old Ismael that went back home. He remembered with sorrow how, twenty-six years ago, he had attacked the Christians in Kamtan with clubs and stones. He had hated them; he even wanted to kill them. But now, when his own life was in danger from Hindu fanatics, it was the Christians who had given him refuge and saved the lives of his family. As he pondered these things, something happened in Ismael's heart. For the first time he began to realize his sin and the love of the Savior.

And then the miracle took place. Shortly after peace was restored in Hyderabad state, David went to Kamtan to meet with the Christian congregation to talk over plans for their new church. Because of their poverty and the cost involved, the Christians had almost given up hope of being able to build their church. Plans were at a standstill. David felt he must offer some encouragement to the congregation.

Their business meeting was suddenly interrupted by the arrival of Ismael and some of his Muslim friends. They stood at the back of the gathering and Ismael asked for permission to speak.

"You may speak, Brother Ismael," David said.

"We have heard," Ismael began, "that the Christians in this village want to build a church in which to worship God. But we also hear there is not enough money because they are all poor people. Now my friends and I are very grateful to them for saving our lives when the Hindus wanted to kill us not very long ago, and we want to show our gratitude to you in a tangible way."

Then he came forward with a garland in his hand—a strange-looking garland—not made of flowers as is usually placed around the neck of one who is honored. He stopped in front of David and placed a garland of *money* around David's neck. "We give this garland of Rupees to you in gratitude. This is to help you build your church. Twenty-six years ago we threw stones on your father's head. Now we want to give you stones for the building of your church!"

The Christians cheered wildly. A totally unexpected gift!

When the money in the garland was counted, it totaled seven hundred Rupees—enough to purchase all needed stones for the new church!

Our Lord had wrought another miracle. Hatred was turned into love. Stones had been turned into a garland.

A year later the new Kamtan Church was dedicated amidst great rejoicing. Ismael was present once again; this time with flower garlands for the missionary and church elders.

This was the first church to be built in Bidar District. Thus, the stones thrown by Ismael and his band of Muslims back in 1922 became foundation stones of the church building program in Bidar district! And Arnett wrote, "Behold what God hath wrought!"

Since that time Ismael has attended the annual Methodist camp meeting at Dharur on many occasions. He has met all three of the "Seamands boys," put his arms about them in a big bear-hug, and garlanded them again and again. Once while J.T. was preaching, Ismael arose and gave witness to his faith in Jesus Christ!

Dharur Jathra and Revival

During his term as superintendent of Bidar District Arnett, in cooperation with fellow missionary M.D. Ross, laid the foundation for his greatest contribution to the spiritual life and evangelistic fervor of South India and Hyderabad Annual Conferences. Two prior life-changing crises, already described, were the chief motivating forces.

First was his experience at Camp Sychar in Mount Vernon, Ohio in the summer of 1912. Since his call to Christian discipleship and missionary service occurred in the atmosphere of an old-fashioned camp meeting, this effective method of evangelism captured his heart and mind. He began to read avidly the history of the camp meeting movement in the United States. An eye-witness account of the famous Cane Ridge, Kentucky, camp meeting of 1801 had a special and lasting influence upon his thinking. Arnett began to ask himself: *Why can't God duplicate such an experi-*

ence even today? And if He can do it in America, why can't He do it also in India?

The second crisis experience was Arnett's infilling with the Holy Spirit on the sidewalk of Clifton Avenue, while a university student in Cincinnati. He was convinced that baptism with the Holy Spirit was the birthright of all believers and an utter necessity for Christian life and service. Furthermore, as a Methodist, it was his heritage "to spread Scriptural holiness throughout the land."

So when the young missionary-engineer arrived in India, two great spiritual ambitions had control of his heart and mind: to inaugurate the camp meeting movement in South India and to witness a repetition of Pentecost in the life of the Indian Church.

In these ambitions he was not alone. At his first Annual Conference session in 1921, he met Rev. M.D. Ross, a few years his senior. Like Arnett, Ross had been converted in a camp meeting in the United States (in Kansas). Like Arnett, he too had trusted in God for his personal Pentecost and believed strongly in the necessity of the Spirit-filled life. This resulted in a David-and-Jonathan-like spirit of friendship, and a Paul-and-Barnabas-like team of evangelism between these two young missionaries. They decided that if they ever found themselves serving in close proximity, they would hold a camp meeting for Indian pastors. Thus, when they were appointed as superintendents of Bidar and Vikarabad Districts adjoining each other, they realized the opportunity had come.

In 1923 Ross and Seamands agreed that they would attempt a miniature camp meeting at a site midway between the two districts. Dates: November 14 to 23. Location: a wooded area between Bidar and Tandur, where there was a large, unused well known as *Bondla Bhavi* (travelers' well).

The strategy was for both missionares to carefully choose and bring from their respective districts the top-level Indian workers, conference members, and local preachers of good experience, along with their wives. Just one aim captured the minds of the two missionaries—to "tarry until" the entire group was filled with the Holy Spirit. They believed that if the main leaders were revived and endued with power, the spiritual impact would be felt throughout the whole ministry and laity as well.

Thus it was that on the opening day of the camp, about one hundred of the district preachers and their wives met together at Bondla Bhavi. A few laymen from nearby villages joined the group, swelling the total number to approximately 150. Some stayed in tents, some built simple brush arbors, others improvised temporary shelters out of bamboo mats. Each family managed its own cooking on outdoor fireplaces. And so the first "jungle camp meeting" was under way.

At first the campers were confused. "What are we doing out here in the jungle?" they asked. "Nothing but tigers and cobras here! What are these crazy missionaries up to anyway? Do they want us to die?"

"Yes," answered the two young missionaries. "We've come here to die. Not in the physical sense, however, but in the spiritual sense."

And soon the campers began to understand as they heard over and over the slogan of the camp meeting: "Die to sin; receive the Holy Spirit; live unto righteousness!"

There were three services a day, with Ross and Seamands alternating as speakers. On the authority of God's Word, backed by personal testimony, the two missionaries expounded "the way of God more perfectly," emphasizing the Christian's obligation and privilege of being filled with the Spirit. No altar call was given, but after each message people were urged to go out alone, under the trees, and pray specifically for baptism with the Spirit. If the assurance of victory came to anyone, he was urged to return to camp and share his personal testimony with the rest of the group.

Nothing happened—for the first three days. But a deep sense of conviction and heart-hunger began to grip the campers. Then on the afternoon of the third day the first victory took place. One of the Telegu-speaking preachers, A.S. Abraham, became so desperate in his search that he sought out Rev. Ross and asked him to come out under a tree and pray with him. Before they arose from their knees, the Spirit came in glorious fulness. That evening Abraham stood in the service and gave a clear-cut testimony to the baptism with the Holy Spirit in his life.

This testimony lit a spark of expectancy in the hearts of others. The next afternoon the second victory took place. Rev. Jotappa Jacob, son of the first convert in Bidar, a conference member, went out to his prayer tree after lunch, determined that he would not return until he had received the Holy Spirit in His fulness. His eyes fell upon the words in Luke 11:13—"How much more shall your heavenly Father give the Holy Spirit to them that ask him?" He closed the Book, bowed his head, and just asked God to give him the Holy Spirit. Suddenly his heart was strangely warmed and Jacob jumped to his feet shouting, "He has come; the Holy Spirit has come!" He ran through the woods looking for someone to tell about what had happened. That evening in the service Jacob shared his testimony with the entire group, and was followed by two other Indian men whom he had led into the new experience during the afternoon.

Other victories quickly followed. Rev. N.S. Samson told the group: "Last night I dreamed or had a vision of a great fire. It started at the missionaries' tent and began to spread until it consumed the whole camp. I thought my brush arbor was on fire. I awoke and all seemed to be light about me. I rushed out and realized it was the fire of the Holy Spirit. Then I prayed that the fire would burn out all the dross in my own heart and that the Holy Spirit would fall on me."

Others began to inquire from these three national leaders. They exhorted and guided people into the experience. Multani, under exhortation of J. Jacob, fell prostrate and began to pray. The Holy Spirit fell on him. Thereafter at dawn he was up every morning, walking through the woods, singing. He became a powerful preacher through the rest of his life.

T.C. Veereswamy, a local preacher, was filled with the Holy Spirit. He was a quiet man, but gave a solid testimony.

Jettiappa of Ganeshpur was an illiterate villager who lived victoriously until his death in 1940.

Jettiappa of Satwar lived only two years after this first camp meeting when the Holy Spirit came to him, but he was a radiant, victorious Christian.

Perhaps the most significant victory, next to Rev. Jotappa Jacob's was that of Rev. Krishnayya, an ordained elder in the Bidar District. He said: "I have studied about the Holy Spirit; I have preached about the Holy Spirit; but never did I realize as now that I have not yet received Him in His fulness. I must receive Him or I cannot live."

Arnett gave him a promise or two from the Word and urged him to go alone into the woods and pray. Before the service was over, Krishnayya returned. The light on his face was the testimony of what had taken place.

And from then on the spiritual fire began to sweep through the camp. Krishnayya and Jacob and Multani formed a great trio and later went out together holding many meetings.

Once started, the blessings continued. Other campers began to form little prayer groups all over the woods.

The missionaries were momentarily pushed into the background. But this is exactly what they had prayed for and longed to see—the Holy Spirit taking possession of the Indian preachers, and the church going forward under their leadership. Now it was no longer a foreign missionary telling what had happened to him in some camp meeting in America; it was an Indian brother telling his own people what had happened to him on Indian soil. This was truly an Indian Pentecost taking place in the twentieth century.

By the end of the week in that historic month of November, 1923, almost every one of the 150 persons present could testify with assurance to the abiding presence of the Holy Spirit.

What took place at Bondla Bhavi was by no means superficial; it was genuine. It was no temporary outburst of emotion; it was a permanent transformation of life. Results were manifest in the lives of individuals and in the spirit of the entire conference. To this very day there are evidences of the permanent results of that first camp meeting throughout the work of South India and Hyderabad Conferences.

When camp broke up on November 23, missionaries Ross and Seamands and the district workers returned to their various places of duty to get ready for district conference. On his way home Arnett began to develop a temperature, and the next day he was delirious with a high fever. The missionary doctor, Dr. Charles Pinckney, diagnosed it as a serious case of typhus. Typhus is an acute infectious disease, characterized by great prostration, severe nervous symptoms, and a peculiar eruption of reddish spots on the body. It is believed that typhus is spread by lice and fleas. (At that time there were plenty of both in the villages.)

Because of Arnett's illness, the Bidar District Conference had to be conducted by his Indian colleagues, Rev. N.W. Samson and Rev. Jotappa Jacob. These two brethren, fresh in their new spiritual experience gained at the camp meeting, were more concerned about spiritual revival than they were about passing resolutions! They both shared their newfound experience with all members of the district conference and urged each one to "tarry until" he was endued with power from the Holy Spirit.

The result was a repetition of what took place at the jungle camp meeting—a new outpouring of the Holy Spirit. Revival fires swept through the group at the district conference and spread out into the district.

Meanwhile, in Vikarabad District nearby where Rev. M.D. Ross was superintendent, a similar movement was taking place. Members of that district conference experienced their personal Pentecost and then went back to their homes and churches to spread the good news.

All this time Arnett was battling for his very life. Annual conference was to take place shortly and he desired so much to be able to attend the conference session and tell the good news of the revival. On his bed he prayed earnestly, "Lord, if You will enable me to go to annual conference, I will bear witness to Your grace."

The Lord said, "I'll raise you up, but when you get to conference you must ask everyone you contact the apostolic question: 'Have you received the Holy Spirit?'"

"Oh, Lord," Arnett answered, "they will say I'm crazy. They'll say the typhus has made me go off my noodle!"

"You can, you must."

"All right, Lord. I'll do it." It was not an easy assignment, but Arnett accepted the challenge.

For twenty-three days he hung in the balance between life and death. During this period he lost thirty pounds, but he held on in faith that God would raise him up to see further evidences of Pentecost. When he was able to get up he was so terribly weak he had to walk with a cane for a while. He was six-feet-one-inch tall, and he weighed only one-hundred-twenty pounds.

Meanwhile, news of the outpouring of the Holy Spirit at Bondla Bhavi camp and at Bidar and Vikarabad district conferences, had spread though the rest of the South India Conference area. So when the members gathered in early January, 1924 at Kolar Town, a strong spirit of expectancy permeated the atmosphere.

An unusual sense of the presence of the Holy Spirit in their midst was felt from the very beginning of the sessions. Delegates from Bidar and Vikarabad began to share their testimony with other delegates. Each evening Arnett and Ross conducted informal prayer-and-witness meetings in the Bible school building.

Remembering the promise made to the Lord, Arnett went from person to person, both missionary and national, and asked the apostolic question: "Have you received the Holy Spirit?" It took a lot of courage to go up to the presiding bishop, Bishop Frank W. Warne, and put the question to him. But the bishop smiled and said, "Yes, Brother Seamands, thank God I have received the Holy Spirit. Hallelujah! I received Him years ago, back in Canada."

The movement of the Spirit at the South India Conference

followed a rather unusual pattern. Each night the Holy Spirit came upon a different *language* group. The first night Telegu-speaking members received their Pentecost; next night, Kanarese-speaking delegates; the third night, Tamil-speaking.

Finally the movement broke through the conference delegation and touched the local Methodist Girls School. Informal services were held nightly in the school hall and many young girls came into a new experience with Christ. In this way the annual conference of 1924 proved to be a great revival conference which brought new spiritual life and power to the leadership of Methodism in south India.

The revival left its lasting impressions upon both missionaries and Indian ministers, so that down through the years South India Conference (now divided into Hyderabad and South India Conferences) has always sought to maintain a high standard of Christian purity and ethics, and to keep evangelism at the very center of its life and work. Spiritual revival has been a keynote of its conference objectives.

Meanwhile, back in the Bidar District, a new phase of the spiritual movement was developing. So far the outpouring of the Holy Spirit had been confined, mostly, to the leadership of the conference—to missionary and ordained preacher. Supply preachers and village laity had not been touched. The latter began to question: "What is the gift of the Holy Spirit? Is this gift only for the American missionary and for the Indian conference member? Is God a respector of persons?" Soon they were to receive God's own answer to their inquiry.

T.C. Veeraswamy was a local preacher who had been present at Bondla Bhavi camp meeting and had received his personal Pentecost. Dad had left the District Training School in this man's hands while he was away at annual conference. Veeraswamy set the training school ablaze with revival and then headed for villages, where, under the inspiration of the Spirit, he developed a technique all his own.

He would select a strategically located village and urge the local Christians to contribute enough rice and rations to feed a large group of people for one day. Then Christians from neighboring villages were invited to join the local group in a one-day revival.

The villagers were requested to be present by early afternoon and were assembled in a shady grove some distance from the village. Veeraswamy gave a simple exposition of the gift of the Holy Spirit, based upon the Scriptures, added his own personal testimony, and then exhorted the people to receive the gift. Three simple steps explained how: die to sin; receive the Holy Spirit; live unto righteousness.

Then the preacher urged each individual to mark out a spot just for himself, fall upon his knees in prayer and *tarry until* he had received assurance of the fulness of the Holy Spirit in his life. (Because of this emphasis of "tarrying until," these meetings came to be known in common parlance as "until meetings.")

By evening the landscape was dotted with individual seekers scattered all across the countryside, and the quiet evening was broken by a volume of petitions ascending unto the Heavenly Father from scores of hungry hearts. Some of the workers walked up and down the hillside, giving special guidance and encouragement to all those who needed counseling. No one was in a hurry; no one looked at the clock. (Clocks were very few.) All tarried until the Spirit came in refining power.

When the very last one had "prayed through," the entire group reassembled and joined in a triumphant procession, marching up and down the hillside, singing and shouting praises to God. Sometimes the procession lasted for two or three hours, breaking up in the early morning hours. Then the group ate their feast of curry and rice and departed for their villages and homes. Veeraswamy went to another village and repeated the procedure.

When Arnett returned from annual conference in Kolar, he learned of this remarkable Spirit-led movement under the direction of Brother T.C. Veeraswamy. He went out into the district in his Model T. Ford to see the sight for himself. In village after village he witnessed these until meetings. Arnett was careful not to take over any direction, but was content to sit by and watch God and His chosen leader carry the movement forward. For now he was seeing with his own eyes the answer to his most earnest prayer. This was Pentecost—in our day—in India—among the simple village folk—in God's own way—and through Indian leadership! Truly God is no respecter of persons or countries. Christ is "the same yesterday, and today, and forever." And the gift of the Holy Spirit is for all!

In this manner, E.A. Seamands and M.D. Ross, who had witnessed the effectiveness of camp meetings as a method of evangelism in the United States, now experienced a demonstration of its effectiveness in their adopted land of India. So they were determined that Dharur Camp Meeting should become an annual affair. Furthermore, it soon became evident to them that the camp meeting, with certain modifications, would easily become indigenous to the life of the Christian Church in India. It appeared to be the exact counterpart of the Hindu *Jathra* (*mela* in North India), a religious institution deeply ingrained in the culture of India.

All across India one can witness great, annual Hindu festivals where countless pilgrims come from miles around to a special place where there is some famous idol or shrine. Most of the jathras, or festivals, are held along the bank of some river or stream. Entire families make the journey together, either by bullock cart or on foot, or by train, and live for a few days camp style out under the trees. They perform their worship at the shrine, carry out their various religious ceremonies, and visit with relatives and friends.

So the idea of a special spot along some stream, where people come together for a religious purpose, fits perfectly with the Indian mind. Thus the camp meeting filled the vacuum in the life of new Christians, most of whom had come from Hinduism and had ceased to attend Hindu jathras after their conversion. The camp meeting soon acquired the name of the "Christian Jathra."

In the third year of the Christian Jathra it was decided to look for a more suitable and accessible location that could become the permanent site of the camp. After much scouting around, the missionaries discovered a pleasant, wooded area on the banks of a small stream just a mile from the little railway station of Dharur, in [the former] Hyderabad State. The mission granted funds to purchase eight acres of this woodlands, and thus Dharur became the home of the camp meeting from then on. "Dharur Jathra" is now a household word in most Christian homes in the Hyderabad area of Indian Methodism.

For several years the annual camp meeting at Dharur continued to be the spiritual powerhouse of South India Conference. It kept fires of evangelism ablaze in the hearts of leaders; it kept the spirit of revival alive in the work of the conference.

But by the year 1933, Dharur Jathra seemed to be dwindling in power and effectiveness. It had become more of an annual preachers' retreat and was no longer penetrating in its outreach. For the next few years Arnett and Ross decided to substitute a series of brief, district-wide gatherings for the one annual camp meeting at Dharur.

Shortly afterward, in 1939, World War II broke out, and restrictions in travel, plus stringent ration regulations, made it extremely difficult to conduct any sort of religious gathering. So during the war years 1939-1945, all such meetings were reluctantly discontinued.

When the war came to an abrupt close in August, 1945, as a result of popular demand it was decided to reinstate Dharur Jathra in November of that year. Attendance was fair, and spiritual results encouraging. The following year J.T. returned to India for his second term and David arrived for his first term of missionary service. From then on for thirteen years, father and two sons were prominent in the program of Dharur Jathra. J.T. served as one of the evangelists every year from 1946 to 1959.

In 1947 the jathra seemed to catch fire. That year the

attendance doubled to become 650; in 1948 it jumped to 1,600; in 1949 to 2,700; and in 1951 to over 5,000. The phenomenal growth of the Jathra in the '70s and '80s will be discussed in a later chapter.

But apart from increase in attendance, there were other significant changes in the jathra. God raised up several Spirit-filled Indian evangelists, who had gifts of preaching and genuine love for people. Among these were Mallappa, a government tax collector, converted in mid-life; and Augustine Salins, a converted high school drawing teacher. Their ministry brought new life to the jathra. Furthermore, the constituency of the camp changed from only Christian worker to laity. The vast majority of those attending consisted of simple village laymen and their families. A host of these villagers heard the Gospel message, surrendered themselves to Christ, and then returned to their villages to witness to their friends and relatives concerning salvation in Jesus Christ.

The impact of this lay witness, backed by transformed lives, soon became evident throughout the area. One day a Hindu village headman met David, and with a puzzled look, asked, "What has happened to your Christians? What kind of idol do you have over there at the Dharur Jathra?"

David tried to explain that there was no idol, only the Presence of the living God. "Well," exclaimed the headman, "I don't know what you've got over there, but since these people have been going to Dharur, something has happened to them. Why, now they're the best people in the village!"

This was the story in village after village. People who went to Dharur had their lives transformed.

Their own testimonies were fascinating. One man held up two leaves and said: "When I went to Dharur I was like this," and he pointed to an old, dried and withered leaf. "Now I am like this," and he held up a fresh green leaf.

Another said, "When I went to Dharur I had three 'demons' inhabiting me—the demons of drink, tobacco, and adultery. But Christ cast out all three demons and set me free!"

Before one of the services, to dramatize Christian experience, a big ditch had been dug and people were asked to cast their sins into the ditch and bury them beneath the sand. One man testified, his face aglow, "Last year when I buried my sins in the ditch, I had peace in my heart. When I got home the tempter came and wanted me to dig them up again, but I just threw more sand on them and they are still buried in that ditch!" Simple, yet sincere testimonies like these found their way into the hearts of many a non-Christian villager and led him to Christ. An evangelistic lay movement was on!

There is little doubt that Dharur Jathra was largely responsible for the spiritual impetus which gave momentum to the group movement which developed in Methodist work in Hyderabad State. The movement was at its height between the years 1947 and 1954. As a result, the number of Christians in Bidar District increased from about 9,000 (in 1924) to about 65,000 today. (The original Bidar District has been split up into three districts.)

And the number of Christians in Methodist sections of the present Karnataka and Andhra States (formerly known as Hyderabad State) has increased from about 40,000 to approximately 250,000 today. The movement has been, for the most part, Spirit-led, and with missionaries and preachers giving inspiration and guidance.

As for Dharur Jathra, in recent years it has given birth to a number of smaller jathras in various parts of India. Several years ago Rev. M.D. Ross was invited by the Nazarene Mission to inaugurate a new jathra in Berar State, in Central India. This jathra has been going on effectively for a number of years now and has become the spiritual powerhouse of the church in that section.

In 1949, while J.T. was superintendent of the Belgaum and Gokak Districts of the South India Conference, it was his privilege to inaugurate a "Western Dharur" along a small stream outside the town of Khanapur. This jathra has initiated a new spiritual movement in that section.

Shortly afterward the World Gospel Mission began a new

Christian jathra of its own near Bangarapet in South India. In addition to these, a score or more of three-day district jathras sprang up throughout Hyderabad and South India Conference areas, some of which attract as many as 8,000 village Christians yearly.

There is little doubt that the jathra has become indigenous to the life of the Indian Church and that it has come to stay.

One facet of Dharur Jathra that has become a beautiful expression of Indian culture is the strong emphasis on Indian music. *Bhajana* (singing praises to God) plays a very important part in Hindu worship. Christians also enjoy expressing their devotion to the living God through bhajana. In city churches most of the hymns sung are translated western hymns, such as "What a Friend We Have in Jesus," "Onward Christian Soldiers," "Sweet Hour of Prayer," and so on. But in jathra—where most participants are from rural churches— no western hymns are used; only Indian lyrics. These consist of Indian-style poetry, in which rhyming is both at the beginning and end of the line, and music based on the classical Indian *ragas* (basic tune patterns).

Indian Christians feel at home with their own style of music and can enter into singing more wholeheartedly. Instead of using an old-fashioned pump-organ or piano, they use their own indigenous instruments— *harmonium* (a reed instrument with two-and-a-half octaves), *thabla* (drums), cymbals, and tambourine. All the people clap their hands in time with the music. Toward the end of the song, the beat picks up considerably; drums and cymbals are played double time, and clapping becomes more pronounced. At the climax the leader raises his right hand and shouts: "Prabhu Yesu Masih Maharaja ki" — "to Jesus the Messiah, Lord and King" — then all the people in the congregation raise their hands and shout "Jai" (victory!). When you have 80,000 joyful Christians singing and shouting at the top of their voices, you get a foretaste of the singing around the throne of God which the Apostle John describes in the Book of Revelation.

Early every morning at Dharur, about 4:30 a.m., groups

of Christians can be heard singing in their tents throughout the entire camp, beginning the day with praises to Almighty God and with prayer. After the evening service, late into the night, bhajana continues as worshippers close the day with thanksgiving to their Redeemer.

Many of these lyrics are composed by Indian pastors and lay people themselves, as an expression of their personal experience with Christ and devotion to Him. Each year several new songs are introduced to the camp, then carried home to hundreds of congregations.

Confrontation at the Cave*

Peace exploded on the mission compound in Bidar one memorable Sunday morning in March, 1924. The spirit of revival was very much in evidence among the Christians—it had continued since Bondla Bhavi. Arnett Seamands was preparing for worship service when suddenly a young man from Mirzapur village pounded on the door. He breathlessly cried, "Sir! A Hindu priest and his wife are in our Prayer Cave! They have buried their idol in the floor! They have written the name of the god *Vitoba* on the wall encircling the idol! What shall we do? They are trying to steal our holy place and make it a Vitoba temple! We are going to gather an army of our Christian students, attack the two in the cave, and throw out the idol! They *cannot* have our Prayer Cave!"

Since their baptism in 1896, Mirzapur Christians, the very first Christians in the area, had used this cave as a sacred meeting place. As new generations came on, a great love for the Prayer Cave permeated the whole area. It became a historic show place—all visitors would be led to this holy spot to hear its story.

The cave was cut back about twenty feet into a rocky red-laterite cliff above the village of Kanarese Mirzapur. In front of the cave was a natural stone platform where several

*by Ruth Seamands. First published in *Good News,* used by permission.

thousands could gather for worship. It was under the supervision of the young Christians of Mirzapur village, a hundred yards away in the valley. In turn, they visited the cave every morning, saw that it was always clean, whitewashed, and that a Bible and hymnbook were kept inside. Now their place was in jeopardy.

Arnett was greatly concerned at this news. But he cautioned, "Go slowly. You know it is a serious offense to 'molest the deity' of another's religion. Come, worship here now, hold steady, and we will pray for God's wisdom."

But there was great turmoil on the compound all day. The young people were ready to fight—and die, if necessary—for their Lord. By the end of the day their strategy had changed. They announced to Arnett, "Sir, all of us young people, and all the school children are going to assemble right in the mouth of the cave and we are going to SING and PRAY until God runs the priest and his wife out! Then we will repossess our cave. God will give us the victory." They dashed off.

Missionary Seamands followed them, climbing the hill to the mouth of the cave. He heard the singing, clapping, and shouting of "Jaya Krist" (victory to Christ!) long before he reached the place. He stood and marvelled at the robust enthusiasm of several hundred children and young people crowding before the cave. The face of the cliff became a loud speaker, broadcasting the clangor far down into the Manjra River valley. Thrilled with their boldness, soon Arnett too, joined in singing Christian songs and shouting, "Jaya Krist!" Some older Christians were also there, their presence giving comfort and strength. For hours the victory songs echoed from the summit, assaulting the ears of the two in the cave.

Suddenly there was a commotion at the mouth of the cave. The Hindu priest and his wife peeked fearfully out the door, looking for a path through the Lord's host of exuberant Christians. With glee the regiment stood back and made way for the two. Down the hill to their village the couple sprinted, as if a hundred demons were chasing them.

The singers milled about—not sure what to do next. Suddenly, with a victorious cry, a Christian carpenter from Mirzapur appeared, cradling a crowbar! Within seconds, the dethroned idol, Vitoba, imbedded in a round, grinding-stone-like base was hauled out the cave door. Again the battalion speedily parted, and god and grindstone rolled down the incline. Then with triumphant clamor, the "army of the Lord" romped down the hill past the helpless god and bivouacked in their village.

But Monday was another faith-testing day. Overnight the priest and his followers had rescued the impotent idol and had reinstated it in the cave floor, the priest beside it. The priest's wife was absent that day, but there were enough of his henchmen gathered nearby to challenge the Christians.

Arnett knew he must stand with the young people, who were already gathering before he heard of it. As he left the house, he grabbed up his old-fashioned camera, thinking to get visible proof of whatever happened. As he approached the cave, the possibility of a big battle was clearly evident. The Lord's army was again in command of the mouth of the cave, singing and shouting. The army of the god of stone stood nearby, muttering angrily. Just as the missionary arrived at the edge of the crowd, several boys entered the cave, brandishing the crowbar. The terrified priest plunged out to join his group.

Rev. Seamands called to his students, "Wait! I want to photograph the idol!"

Seconds later, poor old Vitoba was again kicked down the slope.

At this the priest's hit-men started up, and Arnett turned around to get their pictures. As he aimed the camera at the guerrillas, they suddenly froze in the Indian sun. They had never seen a weapon like that! Thinking the big black box must be some kind of new artillery, they panicked and abandoned Vitoba.

Once again the valley rang with a victory celebration!

Later the "idol group" filed a case in court against the Christians, suing to get "their" cave back. But everyone knew the cave first belonged to the Christians, for Jothappa, who had dug it [page 36], was converted to Christianity. He had started Christian worship in the cave. So the judge threw the case out of court. The judge was a Muslim—and Muslims abhor idols.

Even today the prayer cave plays a very large part in the Christian community. Each Easter morning there is a sunrise service, where hundreds of Christians worship on the hillside in front of the cave. There is singing, praise, preaching, and finally a Communion Service. It is a beautiful and solemn sight as the sun rises with long, red streaks over the jagged hill, to see the large Christian congregation, all dressed in white, worshipping the Lord.

Yes, Easter is an extra special day for the Mirzapur Christians. It's Resurrection, Thanksgiving, and a Hallelujah Day— because the Prayer Cave is theirs!

Let the hills and the caves rejoice . . . Jaya Krist!

3

SECOND TERM – Belgaum and Kolar

In March, 1925, Arnett and Yvonne came home to the States on their first furlough. They spent the year at Grandmother Shields' home in Pittsburgh, Pennsylvania. J.T. was nine, and David four years old at the time.

When they arrived home, the depression had already begun. The Board of Missions in New York was feeling the financial pinch, so they began to cut back on the number of missionaries. The General Secretary said to Dad: "Brother Seamands, we are in financial trouble. We're sorry, but we do not have funds to send you back to India for a second term. We suggest that you take a pastorate here in the States."

Arnett's memory went back to Camp Sychar where he first received his call. He could still see the silver letters etched on red—I-N-D-I-A. His mind also went back to the people he had left in India. They seemed to beckon to him to return.

"My brother," Arnett replied to the Board Secretary, "it was not the Methodist Board that called me to India; it was the Lord. I believe He has resources for our return." So he went from church to church and put his case before God's people. Soon he had sufficient funds for his support. When the General Secretary saw this, he said: "Brother Seamands, you may go back to India. Get your tickets."

One shudders to think how different everything would have been in the South India Conference if Arnett had not taken such a bold stand. We would not be writing this story.

Upon his return to India, Arnett was appointed as evangelist to Belgaum, a city at the extreme western section of South India Conference and about eighty miles from Goa on the coast. British missionaries of the London Missionary Society had started work in Belgaum as far back as 1822. After eighty-two years of ministry they had only a high school, two primary schools, and a Christian congregation of two hundred members. In 1904, they had handed the station over to the American Methodists, who sent Rev. David Ernsberger to supervise it. By 1926 (when Arnett arrived), there were over 12,000 Methodist Christians in the District. The secret of such spectacular growth was this: The L.M.S. missionaries had concentrated their efforts in the city and preached only to the high caste people who, for the most part, were resistant to the Christian message. Methodists went out to villages and preached the Good News to poor, low caste people, who were the responsive segment of Hindu society. They heard the Gospel gladly and came to Christ by hundreds.

Arnett's evangelistic fervor began to make an impact on Belgaum District immediately. His superintendent, Rev J.D. Harris, wrote in the 1926 Annual Report:

> Since Brother Seamands' arrival in March, two camp meetings have been held in the district. Early in the year, Brother E.A. Seamands, assisted by J.H. Garden, selected a place on the banks of the Malaprabha River some eighteen miles from Belgaum. There they had an eight-day meeting with our Indian preachers, teachers, Bible-women and some of the hostel boys. The Holy Spirit was present with power. Brother Garden, writing of this meeting said, 'I have seen many revival efforts by different evangelists, but never since coming to India has my heart been so

gladdened as during our late eight-days camp meeting.'

Arnett arranged for a second camp meeting on the mission compound in Belgaum, for several days preceding the District Conference. He invited Brothers Jacob and Krishnaya from Bidar and Vikarabad, as evangelists and products of the original Bondla Bhavi camp meeting. Concerning these meetings, Superintendent Harris wrote:

> Brother Seamands, because of his knowledge of the language, was able to assist many in their search for peace and forgiveness, and especially among our hostel boys a number found Christ as a real personal Savior. The Holy Spirit was present in great power and manifested Himself mightily in the changed lives of a number of our workers. One Muslim, one Lingayat, and one Maratta [high caste Hindus] were baptized after these meetings.

Numerous boarding school boys were converted that year. Among them were A.R. Bangalore, who later became a pastor and then a district superintendent; Yeshvant Kuri, who became a doctor and earnest Christian witness; and Yargatti Basappa, who served many years in the Kanarese work in Bombay city.

Belgaum, because of its cooler climate (elevation 2,700 feet), was a British military station, and the Methodist Mission held regular Sunday worship services for the non-Anglican soldiers. At that time a Scottish regiment, the H.L.I. (Highland Light Infantry), was stationed in Belgaum. Because of their rough behavior the town people gave them the nickname of "Hell's Little Imps." Around Easter time Arnett conducted a revival meeting for the congregation and a good number of the soldiers were genuinely converted and became zealous witnesses for Christ.

That same year Arnett encouraged several Christian teachers, preachers, and students from Belgaum to attend the annual Christian Jathra at Dharur. He fully intended to escort the group to the Jathra, but on the way he was suddenly stricken with malaria and had to drop out. The spiritual impact of the jathra was soon evident when the delegation returned to Belgaum. Five of the students said their hearts were so full that they simply had to go out and preach to those who had never heard about Christ. One night at eleven o'clock they slipped out of the dormitory "without purse or coat" and were gone for a whole week, teaching and preaching in villages. They were heartily received wherever they went, and people gave them food on their journey. Like John the Baptist, they ate fruits of the jungle and grain of the field to maintain themselves during their absence.

A Green Revolution

Arnett was in Belgaum only a year when the bishop changed his appointment to superintendent of the Bangalore District— 325 miles southeast—with residence in Kolar. Back to where he had first started in 1919!

Bangalore District was far removed from the center of the group movement in Hyderabad State. The Christian community numbered only a few thousand, the majority of whom lived in Kolar. Kolar Congregation itself had a membership of over a thousand. As previously pointed out, there was a thriving English-speaking congregation in Bangalore, made up mostly of Anglo-Indians and a few Britishers working in civil service. There was also a small Kanarese-speaking congregation in Bangalore, another at Bangarapet, and several small rural congregations in villages surrounding Kolar.

Primary emphasis in the district was on institutions. Foremost among these were the before mentioned Baldwin Boys and Baldwin Girls High Schools in Bangalore, which used English as the medium of instruction. The majority of students were from the Anglo-Indian community. In the same city there was a Kanarese- and a Tamil-speaking primary school. Kolar was noted for the Ellen Thoburn Cowen Hospital for Women, and the Industrial Training School which specialized in carpentry and blacksmithy and produced beautiful furniture in teakwood and rosewood. There were also the boys' and girls' hostels, and a Middle School for girls. Within a few years the All-India Tablet Industry at Bangarapet (eleven miles away) was added to the list. Under the direction of Dr. H. H. Linn, the Industry supplied ointments, pills, and many medicines at cost price to all Christian hospitals and dispensaries in India.

Besides general supervision of district work, Arnett's specific assignment was directorship of the Industrial Training School in Kolar. This had been his first appointment when he arrived in India as a lay technical missionary. At that time he had stayed in Kolar only a month before the bishop sent him to Bangalore for language study. This time he was to remain for six years.

As in Bidar District, so also in Kolar. Arnett made a special contribution to the economic status of the surrounding area, this time in the sphere of agriculture. Most rural people were living off the land, and Arnett saw that their farming methods were very backward. For one thing, they used a very crude type of wooden plow, consisting of a piece of wood sharpened to a point and attached to a long handle, drawn by a couple of oxen and guided by hand. So Arnett decided to produce an improved type of metal plow which would do a better job at digging into and turning over the soil. He imported steel plow bottoms from John Deere and Company in the United States, and these were securely bolted to twin iron handles prepared by the blacksmiths in the Industrial School. These were sold to farmers at a price they could easily afford, and so were soon in great demand. They became popularly known as the "Kolar Mission Plough" (British spelling). Every year thousands were sold, and soon old-fashioned wooden plows became obsolete in the countryside around Kolar. Within a few years this widespread use of mission plows sparked a "green revolution" in the area. Crop production increased and the farmers' economic status was lifted.

Once when His Highness the Maharajah (king) of Mysore State was driving through Kolar in his Rolls Royce, escorted by his retinue, he stopped to visit the Mission Industrial School. He wanted to thank Arnett Seamands for his contribution to the agricultural work in Mysore State. In the course of conversation the Maharajah said to Arnett, "Mr. Seamands, please do not patent your Kolar Mission Plough, for it is helping my people tremendously and I want it to be available to all."

Arnett readily agreed. But eventually this proved to be a detriment to the Industrial School, for the government itself started producing the new improved plow at a lower subsidized price. So in a few years the mission plow department was forced out of business. Anyhow, Arnett was not discouraged by this turn of events, for his main objective was not to make a profit, but to help farmers grow more food.

Spirit of Revival

Though Bangalore District was highly institutionalized, Arnett did not allow himself to get bogged down in organization. He always believed that institutions were the *servants* of the Church and *agents* for the Gospel. He was convinced that evangelism is the *primary* task of the Church in all departments. Thus he injected an evangelistic spirit into every activity of the district.

In his very first year in Kolar, he started a new camp meeting, or jathra, in a wooded area near Garnahalli, a village about four miles out of Kolar. This jathra was held annually for a number of years. Regarding the first camp, Arnett wrote in his 1927 report:

> All the Indian preachers, Bible women, teachers, several missionaries, and from time to time others, some hundred or more people, gathered in a pretty grove for six days, to tarry day and night for an outpouring of the Holy Spirit. Many were truly blessed, and God visited those who were truly in earnest about the salvation or sanctification of their souls. From this place of power the workers divided into three bands and went out through the length and breadth of our field, proclaiming Jesus Christ as

Savior. As a result of this Gospel campaign of intensity, four-teen souls in a new village were led to Christ and received baptism.

One year the British principal and the Indian vice-principal (Rev. Preston and Rev. Gurushanta), along with sixteen students of the Union Kanarese Seminary at Tumkur, attended the camp meeting and were greatly blessed. Thus Arnett rejoiced in his 1930 report:

> A remarkable spiritual uplift came to our friends, and several unmistakably received the Holy Spirit. They went away testifying that in the Seminary they were taught *about* the Holy Spirit, but there under the trees they had been baptized *with* the Spirit.

Each year at District Conference time a ten-day revival meeting was held at Kolar. All Indian pastors were present to participate in the services. An endeavor was made to spiritually quicken all phases of the work at one time. A quartet of evangelists were invited in to help, so that services could be held separately in the two schools, the workshop, church, hospital, and among the Bible women. Arnett explained what happened:

> After a few days of foundation laying, the inward work of the Spirit began to be outwardly manifest and souls began to pray through in all quarters. Day and night the Spirit's work was manifest, and by the end of the battle a considerable number of both young and old sought the Savior in the remedying of their soul-needs to real satisfaction. Some were truly saved, and others were definitely sanctified. Some young men were called of God to preach His glorious Gospel to their own people.

Each year the month of March was set apart for a concentrated evangelistic effort to penetrate the villages all around. This was an ideal time to reach the people, because they are idle between one harvest and seed re-sowing time.

Every November several missionaries and Indian pastors went in groups to attend the conference-wide jathra at Dharur. They returned with quickened spirits and a new concern for revival in their own districts.

As a result of all these evangelistic efforts, there were several converts in the Kolar area, some of whom were high caste Hindus. One was a young man of twenty, Ram Achari, from the goldsmith caste. He requested public baptism in his own village in view of his relatives and friends. One was a Brahmin who had been converted to Islam while in the University and was a public lecturer on Islam. He attended one of the revival services, was convicted of his sin and accepted Christ as his personal Savior.

A special attempt was made to reach the Muslims who constituted a sizeable majority of the Kolar populace. Concerning these efforts Arnett wrote in the 1930 report:

> Three times during the year special services in Urdu for Muslims have been held and hundreds have crowded our church. On one occasion the place was jammed and the very windows were full. Meetings lasted hours and about a dozen have come forward stating that they desire to follow Christ. These are being followed up, and may the Lord give many souls from this group.

Bangalore also came in for its share of revival. Each year a week-long preaching mission was conducted in the Richmond Town Methodist Church, for the spiritual benefit of the congregation as well as students of the two Baldwin Schools. Several visiting evangelists from the United States were greatly used by God in those meetings. Among them were the Rev. Miss Willa D. Caffray, Dr. and Mrs. Ridout, and the famous Asbury Trio consisting of Eugene Erny, Virgil Kirkpatrick, and Byron Crouse. When that trio came, Dad was acting as pastor of the Richmond Town Methodist Church, and in his 1931 district report he gave an eye-witness account of the meetings:

Nine days at Easter-tide were times of true revival in the English Church when the Asbury Trio campaigned in our midst. In fact, this series of evangelistic meetings proved to be a stir from above to much of the Cantonment. These three young men came to us Spirit-filled "in the fullness of the blessing of the Gospel," and Bangalore began to be turned upside down. At least three hundred souls must have sought the Savior at the public altar of prayer for either pardon or holiness. The results of this visitation from on high are still manifest amongst us in various ways and the future is bright indeed for a glorious work. A new development in the form of an after-dinner Sunday night sing-song service has arisen and it is not an infrequent sight to see two hundred or more out at this late hour service of deep blessing.

A great number of students from the Baldwin Schools surrendered their lives to Jesus Christ during this revival and became zealous witnesses for the Master. One of the young men was Jack Finch, who later went on to Leonard Theological College and became pastor of Bowen Memorial Methodist Church in Bombay. Then he came to the United States and earned the Ph.D. degree in psychology and counseling. Through his influence a gift of over a million dollars was granted to Fuller Theological Seminary, and the department of psychology was opened on campus.

It was through the influence of the Asbury Trio that J.T. and David were led to Asbury College in Wilmore, Kentucky, when the time came for their undergraduate studies. Also through the influence of Byron Crouse, both J.T. and David were inspired to learn to play the trombone.

In addition to his emphasis on evangelism, Arnett also gave much support to the institutions in the Kolar-Bangalore area. He supervised building a new Nurses' Training School, the Baby Fold, and Tuberculosis Ward in the E.T.C.M. hospital in Kolar. He opened a new department of motor mechanics in the Industrial School, and a branch repair shop in the Kolar Gold Fields. He was also instrumental in bringing the All-India Tablet Industry (to make medicines) from Vikarabad to

Bangarapet, eleven miles from Kolar. Down through the years this industry has proved a great blessing to medical work all over India, and to missions of all denominations. During this time the Baldwin Boys School was suffering from a heavy debt and financial crisis, which almost forced closing its doors. When Arnett was asked to take over the Richmond Town Church as a part-time pastor in 1931, at the same time he was district superintendent and director of the Industrial Training School. He suggested that the amount being raised by the congregation for pastoral support be turned over to the Boys School. Thus, money from the church to the school paid all interest on the schools' debt, and this arrangement actually saved the school. Today it is a flourishing institution with over a thousand students and excellent facilities.

Too Many Monkeys

During Arnett's term in Kolar an unusual event took place. Because of his standing in the community, Arnett was asked to serve on the town council, a rare experience for a foreigner. At one of the official meetings, a Muslim member complained because of the increase of the monkey population in town, and of the nuisance it was causing. "Just recently," the councilman said, "a monkey jumped on my daughter and snatched some candy out of her hand, severely scratching her in the assault. This is getting too dangerous," he shouted. "We must do something about this situation! I suggest we hire someone to shoot all the monkeys."

There was an instant loud protest from Hindu members of the council—they were in the majority—for they worshipped monkeys in the form of Hanuman, the Monkey King. "No!" they shouted back, "you can't kill our monkeys. They are sacred to us!"

"Well then," suggested the Muslim, "let's hire some people to catch the monkeys in cages, transport them to a nearby jungle, and let them loose."

The Hindus thought for a while. "That won't do, they

countered. "You must remember that these are *civilized* monkeys. They have lived in the city for a long time. They are not used to jungle life. If you turn them loose in the trees of the forest, suddenly a tiger or two will come along and let out a deep growl. The monkeys, unaccustomed to such a strange sound, will get so scared that they will lose their grip on the tree branch and fall to the ground, only to be devoured by the tigers."

The argument continued and nothing was settled. Finally, when monkeys increased at such a rate that the situation became desperate, Kolar Council as a whole agreed to transport the monkeys a few miles out of town and let them loose. But of course, in a few months they all came back to Kolar.

A sequel to this story is that after the monkeys had been deported, plague broke out in Kolar—the first plague in several years. Many people died because of that dreaded disease. Then the Hindu people in town began to say: "See, we told you so! We mistreated our gods and now we are being punished!"

4

THIRD TERM — Raichur and Yadgiri

In March, 1933, Arnett and Yvonne came to the States on their second furlough. They made their home with Mrs. Shields, Yvonne's mother, who had moved to Wilmore, Kentucky, to provide a home for David to complete high school, and for J.T. to enroll in Asbury College. As mentioned previously, Mrs. Shields had stayed in India several years to provide a home for her two grandsons while they were students in the Baldwin Boys School in Bangalore.

For a year and a half Arnett was busily engaged in deputation work in the churches at home, and then in 1934, he and Yvonne returned to India for their third term of service. The bishop appointed Arnett superintendent of two adjoining districts—Raichur and Gulbarga, with residence in Raichur. But before proceeding to describe his ministry in this area (the problems he faced and solutions he sought), it is necessary to provide some background information about the situation in which he found himself upon arrival in Raichur.

The original group movement in the South India Conference area took place between 1905 and 1925. (In 1925, the conference was divided to form a second area—the Hyderabad

Annual Conference.) During that twenty-year period, Methodist Christian constituency grew from 3,991 to 78,745, an average of 3,748 baptisms each year. It was an exciting time of advancement for the church.

Then around 1925, economic depression began to hit the United States and to seriously affect Christian work in India. Apportionments were drastically reduced, and the number of personnel—both missionary and Indian—was cut almost in half. As a result, the conference leaders decided not to baptize in any new villages, for with the depleted ministerial staff they would not be able to adequately shepherd and nurture such a vast number of new converts. Instead, they resolved to consolidate gains of the past two decades. They would not make new Christians; they would help existing Christians to become better Christians.

Results of this policy were tragic. The group movement came to a sudden stop; evangelistic spirit of the conference died; morale of the church was at a low ebb. Not only did the leaders fail to consolidate their position, they actually lost ground. By 1935, there were four thousand *less* Christians in South India-Hyderabad areas than there were ten years previously.

During his first term of service in India, when Arnett had served as superintendent of Bidar District, the group movement was at its height. Thousands were entering the Church each year. During the period of "consolidation," however, he was ministering in the Kolar-Bangalore area, which was far removed from the center of the group movement. He was not able to observe personally the results of this new policy. So when, in the fall of 1934, Arnett arrived at his new post, he was shocked to see the spiritual condition of rural congregations, particularly in Gulbarga District. Out of 265 congregations, 170 were without any pastoral supervision whatsoever; the remaining 95 had only partial oversight. One village Christian pictured the sad state of affairs when he exclaimed, "I was baptized as a mere lad. Now I am the father of two children and have scarcely seen a preacher in the interim.

What a good Christian I might have become if I had received instruction through all these years!"

"This ghostly and ghastly situation," wrote Arnett, "has haunted me all through the year. It ought to also haunt the entire South India Conference." He was determined to remedy the situation as best he could, and soon.

Strategy for Renewal

The solution, Arnett decided, was two-fold: first, to re-vitalize the spiritual life of the pastors and laity, and second, to reoccupy neglected villages with new personnel.

To achieve the first objective, Arnett inaugurated a chain of sectional jathras culminating in the district jathra at Yad-giri, an important town in the center of the area.

In 1936, seven three-day camps were held over the two districts. These were conducted over week-ends in strategic centers, with hundreds in attendance at each place. Not only did Christians turn out in great numbers and were greatly revived in spirit, but an average of five delegations of enquir-ers from new villages came to each camp, either to make re-quests for Christian instruction or to announce that they had already decided to follow Christ. This was evidence of new spiritual life in the congregations.

The second objective—to reoccupy neglected villages and evangelize new areas—demanded a bold new revolutionary strategy. The main difficulty was a financial and labor prob-lem. Early missionaries had made no plan for self-support all these years. They took the attitude that the low caste Chris-tians were too poor to give, so they wouldn't ask them to give to the support of the Church. Consequently all salaries of the Indian personnel were paid by mission funds from America. Then when the great depression hit the United States, the Board of Missions and the Conference lost much of their financial resources. Many missionaries were requested to take pastorates at home, and many Indian pastors were laid off from the ministry. Between 1925 and 1935 the num-ber of missionaries in South India Conference decreased from

48 to 32, and the Indian staff dropped from 637 to 313. All this happened in the face of tremendous receptivity to the Gospel on the part of low caste Hindu people. Thus, in the words of Jesus, "the harvest truly was great, but the laborers were few."

To remedy the situation Arnett outlined a five-fold plan to:

1. Emphasize the principle of stewardship and tithing for all Christians.

2. Encourage existing congregations to assume full support for their pastors.

3. Open a Training School in Raichur to prepare pastor-teachers for a self-supporting ministry.

4. Baptize new converts on condition that they would support their pastor.

5. Train village lay-leaders to assist pastors on a voluntary basis.

Several steps were taken immediately to implement this plan. At every Christian wedding ceremony, the couple was challenged to give a tithe of the wedding expenses toward pastoral support. Each family was assigned a "quota" for giving, in accordance with their financial status. Village parents were asked to pay a nominal monthly fee for their children in the boarding school (previously they paid nothing). An annual Lay Leaders Training Institute was held for two or three days in each of the two districts, to give instruction in such subjects as stewardship, self-support, Christian customs and worship. One year, 154 leaders from 52 different villages attended the institute and greatly benefited from the instruction and discussions. In addition, village pastors and teachers were encouraged to conduct adult literacy classes, using the newly prepared Laubach charts, so that people would be able to read the Bible and develop their spiritual lives. In one congregation of twenty-five members, every person from the age of seven to fifty-five years, both men and women, learned to read within a few months.

In 1936 Gulbarga District was divided to form a new district, Yadgiri, and Arnett was appointed superintendent. He maintained residence in Raichur and served as district missionary of that district. Progress was made during the next few years, but many problems had to be faced.

The self-support program suffered severely from a lack of enthusiasm on the part of the preachers themselves. They preferred the old system of mission subsidy for they could count on receiving their salary regularly on the first of each month. It gave them a sense of security. They were reluctant to step out on faith and depend on the offerings of their "poor members."

The year 1938 proved to be an especially difficult one. Due to failure of the monsoon rains, famine stalked the district for several months. Large groups of people migrated with their cattle to distant, more favored areas. Many Christian congregations were simply not at home for months. As a result, the self-support program suffered a serious setback, for people had little or nothing to give. The drought also necessitated cancellation of all regional jathras and the annual Village Lay Leaders Training Institute. Furthermore, because of lack of personnel, Arnett was again asked to take over supervision of the Industrial Training School in Kolar. Regarding this assignment Arnett wrote in his report:

> My personal share in this battle this year has been seriously limited due to the half-time shuttle schedule between Raichur and Kolar. I have tried to faithfully serve one Master, but I have found it very crippling business to try to serve two mission stations 300 miles apart.

Nevertheless, in spite of all these obstacles, Arnett was privileged to witness progress on several fronts. As a result of the evangelistic campaigns, there was a new spirit of revival among the Indian personnel; many received the fullness of the Holy Spirit. Village Christians learned to give more generously and systematically, and the level of self-support was raised. Several new Indian pastors were added to the district staff, and baptisms took place in many new villages.

Lay leaders began to assume greater responsibility in spiritual oversight of the congregations.

Victory in Bhimanhalli

What happened in the strategic village of Bhimanhalli was especially impressive. Low-caste people of this village had been hearing the Gospel off and on for several years, but had never seriously considered following Christ. Then a series of events seemed to make them desperate for a better life, and they decided that Christ offered the only ray of hope for the future.

One day while Arnett was meeting with the district preachers at Yadgiri, his attention was arrested by a long line of thirty-five men filing into the mission compound. Weary and worn by a long hot day's walk, they declared with one voice that they were from Bhimanhalli and represented fifty-five families there, all of whom had settled in their hearts to become Christians. "When will the missionary come personally to the village?" they asked.

Arnett said he would try to get to Bhimanhalli within two weeks, but urgent matters prevented him from going. A few weeks later a second delegation walked to Yadgiri, strongly urging the missionary to visit their village soon. Arnett said that he could probably make the trip the following week, but again circumstances hindered his going.

Then one day Arnett was working at his desk in Raichur, sixty miles away, when the postman brought a letter from the assistant district superintendent in Yadgiri. He had written in haste: "Eight men from Bhimanhalli are here sitting on my doorstep. They declare they will camp here and fast unto death until Mr. Seamands gives them a fixed date for his visit."

"I'll be there Friday!" Arnett wrote back immediately.

Bhimanhalli, at that time, was an isolated village, just beyond a small jungle. Arnett and some of his colleagues made the tedious journey by camel. By the time they got there, from hours of sitting on the hard backs of camels, they were suffering from a severe case of *seat*-sickness. Upon arrival, they were met by a procession of a hundred people, and jubilantly escorted into town by a corps of drummers. The booming of those large drums sounded like a volley of big guns.

Arnett and his group stayed several days. During this time the Gospel was proclaimed uncompromisingly to these eager inquirers. Men, women, and children flocked to hear the good news of the Savior. Repentance for sin, forsaking the old ways, and faith in Jesus Christ as personal Savior—these were constant themes of the messages. People responded with true contrition and faith, and asked for a pastor to be assigned to them. Arnett agreed to their request on condition that they assume full support of the pastor. They accepted the terms, and within a few days Rev. H.G. Mitra, a recent seminary graduate, along with his wife and baby moved in to shepherd them. It was the first time that a congregation accepted full financial responsibility for their pastor from the very beginning. Arnett called it his "grand experiment."

Within a month after Rev. Mitra's arrival, Bhimanhalli people rallied to his call, tore down the village shrine, carried baskets full of mud, wood, brass, and copper idols, and threw them on the village dump heap. It was goodbye to idolatry! Six months later, after intensive instruction and guidance in the Christian faith, Arnett had the glorious privilege of baptizing over 400 new believers in Bhamanhalli on the day before Easter. Easter Sunday itself was a great feast day, with much singing and rejoicing.

Yvonne's Part

While Arnett was out in evangelistic work in villages, Yvonne, with the help of her servants, kept all wheels of the mission compound oiled and running smoothly. She was in charge of the boys' hostel with about one hundred boys. She had to oversee buying all supplies, health, and the larger discipline problems. These boys were from villages, where sanitation was not known, so they had to be taught. Often when boys arrived their bodies were covered with sores of itch. These had to be scrubbed until the scabs were all cleaned off and then salve was applied. Malaria, worms, head lice, and dysentery were all problems, along with the ever-present snakes, scorpions, heat, and dust.

But Yvonne kept a beautiful home, provided bountiful food for all who came, and kept Arnett going healthy and strong.

Her hospitality was well known. In January, 1941, she took seven young, new OMS missionaries into her home in Raichur, India. J.T. and Ruth were two of them. The missionaries stayed for several weeks, learning about India, studying Scriptures, and praying, trying to find the will of God as to where they should begin their missionary work. Feeding seven hungry Americans was no easy task on a mission compound hundreds of miles away from a good meat and vegetable supply. But Yvonne coped with all difficulties with joy. She had her son J.T. back in India! And he had brought his new bride whom she had not met before.

Mrs. Lettie B. Cowman, author of *Streams in the Desert* and co-founder of the Oriental Missionary Society, wrote to Yvonne concerning her generosity:

> I do not feel we are strangers although we have never met. It was such a joy to have your beloved son and daughter-in-law with us here [in Los Angeles] for the very brief time before they sailed away for our beloved India. We fell in love with them and prophesy a very great future before them.
>
> It was so kind of you to open your great heart and your beautiful home to house our missionaries. I wish to sincerely thank you and may the Lord Himself abundantly reward you for your loving kindness toward them.
>
> May I send you my little book "Streams in the Desert." I trust you will find something helpful in its pages. I don't know that I will ever be able to make a journey to India as I am not quite as youthful as Ruth, but you will have a furlough someday

and then, God willing, I wish to have the joy of having you in my home in California.

Again my very sincere thanks to you and your husband for all the many acts of kindness shown to our India missionary group.

Yours in His blessed fellowship,
Lettie B. Cowman
July 3, 1941

The Story of Shankarappa

During his ministry in the Raichur-Yadgiri sector, Arnett made the acquaintance of an outstanding Christian lay leader, B. Shankarappa. Several years previously, Shankarappa and his family, along with two brothers and their families, were among a group of one hundred new believers who had been baptized in the village of Yellari, about twenty-five miles from Yadgiri. The transformation of these three men was genuine from the start. When they were converted they took their household idols and pulverized them to dust. They valiantly opposed sin in any form. Furthermore, their new life in Christ gave them a new sense of dignity and ambition. Through hard work and thrift, in the course of time the three brothers were able to acquire 120 acres of land from the high caste people in town. They tore down their joint mud huts and erected a substantial new stone house and also built a work house in the middle of the field. In this way they broke the shackles of poverty and became fairly well-off financially. For an "untouchable" family, this was indeed a major accomplishment.

Shankarappa, eldest in the family, became a very effective witness for Christ throughout the district. He was a Christian puritan, strongly opposed idolatry, and openly challenged the common superstitions of the Hindu village people. For instance, when building a house, it is a Hindu practice for divisions between rafters to be of an odd number—three, five, or seven, etc. A feeding trough for animals in the barn must run cross-wise to the rectangle. No pillars must stand opposite to a door or window. The fireplace must be in the north end of the house. Christian Shankarappa shocked his Hindu neighbors by laughing at the curse of the gods, and in each of these instances constructed his new house exactly contrary to the "rules." "See," he said to the onlookers, "my house will stand just as firm as yours."

Each year non-Christian farmers consult an astrologer for the auspicious day of the week to sow their seed. The wiseman/astrologer studies the stars and declares, for instance, "Wednesday is the day. Sow then and great will be your harvest." (He then walks off with a handsome fee.) Shankarappa would wait until the declaration was broadcast over the neighborhood and then declare boldly, "My friends, I will sow my seed on Thursday! See if you have a better harvest than mine."

Shankarappa traveled from village to village, bearing his witness to the transforming power of Jesus Christ, and challenging his outcaste people to put their trust in the Savior. He was the main influence in winning a large number of people to Christ in many new villages, including Bhimanhalli that was just mentioned.

Arnett met Shankarappa when he first visited Yellari in February, 1935. They soon became the best of friends. But strange as it may seem, for some reason or other, Shankarappa had a prejudice against the jathras that Arnett started throughout the district. For four years he stayed away from them. Then in February, 1939, probably out of sheer curiosity, he attended the camp meeting at Yadgiri. Two lay evangelists from the States, Miss Anna McGhie and Miss Annie Laurie Granier, were speaking primarily on the subject of the Holy Spirit. Shankarappa, now in his late sixties, responded to the invitation and tarried for the fullness of the Holy Spirit. Then he was fired with a new zeal and became even more effective for the Lord. Concerning this transformation Dad wrote in a printed letter to friends back home:

> Shankarappa then insisted on following me on a full twelve-day tour. What gracious spiritual times our party enjoyed!

Brother Shankarappa became the leading preacher of the group, exhorting Christians to "be filled with the Spirit" and non-Christians to turn to Christ alone for salvation. One night after meeting we retired after midnight—all but this zealous brother. Late in the night I was aroused from my slumber by someone in conversation. It was our brother exhorting another to trust Christ with his whole heart. The time: 2:15 a.m. The talk continued another hour.

As a result of Shankarappa's work on this tour, an open door into the hearts of hundreds of "untouchables" in four new villages came to pass. Such personal work is the high hope of Christ's Kingdom coming to India!

The greatest victory, however, occurred in Shankarappa's own village of Yellari. When he and his brothers had been baptized many years previously, only a portion of the *keri* (outcaste section of the village) had come to Christ. All these years many of his relatives and neighbors had held out against the Gospel, in spite of strong witness in word and life from Christian families. After his infilling with the Holy Spirit, Shankarappa became bolder in his witness to this non-Christian group. Arnett said, "Shankarappa ripened in radiance like a big Indian mango basking out in the tropical sun."

In May, 1940, a genuine revival broke out in the keri. Shankarappa called all the people together, and like Joshua of old, challenged them to make up their minds. "How long," he cried out, "how long will you halter between two opinions? Choose this day whom you will serve. Choose between life and death!" Within a short time a total of three hundred persons, comprising sixty different families, were baptized and joined the Yellari Church. The entire keri was now one-hundred-percent for Christ. Not long afterward a school and dispensary were opened and a fine church building erected. The congregation went on full support for their pastor. Yellari became a model Christian community for the whole district.

All this made a tremendous impact on the rest of the South

India Conference, so that at its regular session in December, 1939, the assembly passed a resolution that all districts should follow the "Raichur-Yadgiri Plan." They scrapped the policy of "consolidation" which they had followed in the previous decade, and issued a call for advance on all fronts! The group movement in the various districts was thus revitalized. Whereas between 1925 and 1935 the Christian constituency in South India Conference had *decreased* by approximately 1,500, between 1935 and 1945 it *increased* by almost 9,000. Arnett's influence kept fires of evangelism burning throughout the whole conference area.

During this term Arnett's heart was gladdened by the arrival of two new recruits on the field. The first was in the person of Mr. Hendrix Townsley, graduate of the University of California at Berkeley, in mechanical engineering, and graduate of Asbury Theological Seminary in Wilmore, Kentucky. While at Berkeley Mr. Townsley had responded to an invitation during a summer camp and had volunteered for full-time Christian service overseas. Though he did not feel a specific call to any particular field, Hendrix leaned toward serving somewhere in Africa, perhaps the Congo. So he studied French while in seminary, to prepare himself for the field.

When Arnett was on furlough in 1934 and living in Wilmore, he had made the acquaintance of Hendrix Townsley, and immediately became interested in him because of his background in engineering. So he talked to him about the possibility of going out to India. Then when Arnett came back to the States in 1936 as a delegate to General Conference, he brought news from the field that Dr. H.H. Linn had just opened the All-India Tablet Industry in Bangarapet and desperately needed a helper. The doctor was willing to pay Hendrix's travel out to India and guarantee his salary for the next three years. Hendrix thought it was wise to have an official connection with the Board of Missions in New York, so he applied and was accepted for the position in Bangarapet. On November 2, 1936, he sailed for India.

Rev. Hendrix Townsley worked in the Tablet Industry for a while, then assisted Arnett in the Industrial School at Kolar, and finally took over complete charge of the school. Later he served as superintendent of Raichur and Yadgiri Districts, and then was transferred to North India as superintendent of Delhi District. During his 37½ years of service in India, Rev. Townsley superintended the building of Holston Hospital in Yadgiri (1955), and the construction of Centenary Methodist Church in New Delhi. He also helped in building several village churches. Arnett always looked upon Hendrix as "one of his boys" and took great pride in the fact that he had steered this fellow engineer toward South India Conference.

The other person to arrive on the field just before Arnett left on his third furlough was his eldest son J.T., who, along with his wife, Ruth, arrived in India in February, 1941.

In Dangerous Waters

Dad and Mother packed for their furlough toward the end of 1941. They were due to sail on a Dutch ship from Bombay some time in early November. We do not know the exact intended date of departure, but when they arrived in Bombay to board the ship, there was a problem. Some mechanical difficulty had caused the ship to be put into drydock for repairs.

They waited in the missionary guest house for two weeks, anxious to get to America. They needed a furlough after six years in the heat of the Deccan, and Mother, especially, was more than a little put out with the delay.

Finally, on November 20, 1941, they were able to board and the ship steamed out of Bombay, down around the southern tip of India, then eastward toward Surabaya in Indonesia. There they stopped for a few days to take on passengers and supplies.

On the morning of December 7, 1941, while still in port, Dad came up from his cabin and met the Captain on deck. The Captain greeted Dad and then said to him, "Reverend Seamands, this morning Japan bombed Pearl Harbor and many of your ships and planes were destroyed, and many Americans killed. The United States has now declared war on Japan. Now your country and my country are at war on the same side."

"Pearl Harbor!" Dad exclaimed. "Isn't this the very morning that this ship was supposed to put in at Pearl Harbor?"

"Yes. We would have been there when the Japanese attacked, if we had not been held up in Bombay for repairs."

"Thank God for repairs!" Dad said fervently.

Later the Captain called everyone on board to a meeting in the lounge. He announced, "Now that war has been declared, this ship cannot proceed on her planned course, which would have taken us via Singapore, Hong Kong, Hawaii, and over to California. Also, we must institute wartime measures aboard this ship. I am asking everyone of you to turn in all maps you have, of any kind. There will be no daily newspapers aboard as is the usual custom. This ship will observe total blackout at night. Absolutely no smoking on deck. Every porthole will be sealed at night. My crew has orders not to tell anyone where we are or what our course is, for reasons of safety. I cannot tell you when we will leave Surabaya. Turn in your maps to the purser, please. That is all."

They stayed in port in Indonesia for two more days, and on the third night, December 10, 1941, at 3:00 a.m., the ship's engines started up. When daylight came passengers could tell by the sun that they were headed south. They kept going south day after day, and the weather got colder and colder. Then they turned east and stayed on that course for many days. Dad figured out that they were going under Australia and New Zealand, and were headed for the southern tip of South America. He was right. Nearing the tip of Chile, the ship turned straight north, finally putting into port at Los Angeles. A two-month voyage of 20,000 miles! But God had been with them.

They had been at sea when their first grandchild was born. Sylvia Ruth, daughter of J.T. and Ruth, was born December 26, 1941 in Kolar Hospital. After landing, Dad and Mother heard the news from Ruth's brother, Arthur Childers, who was living in Los Angeles. Mother was delighted. She had always wanted a girl!

Six months later Ruth brought the baby home by another ship. The United States Consul had ordered all Americans to evacuate India, and had provided a ship, the S.S. Brazil. That trip took six weeks, in total blackout with some hair-raising escapes and a severe epidemic of measles on board. J.T. stayed in India in spite of the order; he felt God wanted him to stay and help start a Bible school.

When Ruth first arrived in Wilmore with baby Sylvia, Mother and Dad, Grandma Shields, Ruth and the baby all rented rooms in the seminary building. At that time Asbury Theological Seminary had only one building—Larabee-Morris. Mother, Dad, and Grandma lived on the second floor near the classrooms, and Ruth and the baby had a room downstairs on first floor. Ruth enrolled for some seminary classes and Mother and Grandma helped with the baby.

Everything was in that one building—dormitory rooms, class rooms, lounge, dining hall, and kitchen. The kitchen and dining room were on the first floor, and Mrs. Oliver, a great saint of God, was head of that department. She was a mighty prayer warrior, and when she felt the need to pray she got down on her knees in the middle of the kitchen.

More than once, I (Ruth), whose room was right next to the kitchen, would smell something burning and hear prayers ascending. I'd run to the kitchen and there would be Mrs. Oliver on her knees, her face raised toward heaven, praising the Lord, shouting and praying. She'd be shaking the very gates of the Kingdom, oblivious to lunch burning on the stove.

But Dad often said, "What a blessing to have a sanctified cook!"

We later moved to a house on Kenyon Avenue in Wilmore, where Grandma Shields died in November of 1943.

Grandma Shields had been a great bulwark for the Seamands family. She had spent the last twenty-five years of her life making a home for her two grandsons, both in India and in the United States. They had actually lived much longer with her than with their parents, and they greatly loved her. She was much respected in the Wilmore community, and baby Sylvia adored her. Just before her death (from a heart attack) she wrote to J.T. still in India:

> My darling J.T.,
>   This is goodbye. I'm going up to be with Jesus.
>   Your little Sylvia is so sweet.
>   Stick to the old Book and preach the Word.
>   Meet me in heaven.
>
> Love,
Grandma.

It was nearly three years before J.T. could get home to be reunited with his family. Not until July, 1944, could Mother and Dad return to India. Dad used this time to travel extensively in U.S.A. from church to church, trying to inspire support for the work in India.

**Young missionaries — Arnett and Yvonne Seamands
in Bangalore, India, with their son J.T., 1921**

A beautiful church—Thatha's design. The Gulbarga Methodist Church

Thatha's home office.
At least ten handwritten letters each day

"Crossing into the Promised Land" on the
way to Dharur Jathra

Bishop Elia Peter wrapping Thatha in a shawl of honor, 1983

Seamands Family in India. Left jeep: Helen, David,
Stephen, Sharon, and Deborah. On middle jeep:
J.T's family: Sheila, Sandy, Ruth, Sylvia, J.T.
On right jeep, Yvonne, Arnett. 1954

Women in Arnett's Life:
Grandmother Ida E. Shields,
Yvonne, Ruth, and Baby Sylvia,
when they lived in the seminary
building, 1942

Yvonne and Arnett, 1976

Takeoff for India, 1963

**Indian garlands —
smothered in love**

**Three stalwarts of the Gospel:
Alex Reid, E.A. Seamands,
J.C. McPheeters**

Thatha loved Ichthus, the Christian rock festival held every year in Wilmore. At age 75 he played his Indian cymbals and praised the Lord with other Ichthus enthusiasts

5

GOD'S ENGINEER

It has already been pointed out that the great group movement toward Christ in the South India Conference area was at its height between 1905 and 1925. During that twenty-year period the Christian constituency increased from 3,991 to 78,745. In Bidar District alone during the three years that Arnett was superintendent (1922-1925), 4,241 new converts were baptized and incorporated into the church.

When the financial depression began in the United States in 1925, it seriously decreased the number of missionary and Indian personnel in South India Conference. As a result the group movement came to a halt for the next ten years, but then in 1935 it suddenly took hold again. So by 1940, there were over 82,000 Methodist Christians in the Hyderabad jurisdiction.

Thus a new and urgent need was manifest in the conference. There were now hundreds of new Christian congregations scattered throughout rural districts. They were active worshiping and witnessing units of believers, founded on preaching the Word and administering the Sacraments.

But they were all lacking in one point: they had no church building in which to gather for worship. Congregations had to assemble on the veranda of some village house, or in the street in front of their homes, or out under some shady trees. Passing bullock carts, dust of the roads, and an occasional knock-down-drag-out dog fight all added to the confusion during services.

Sordidness of such surroundings detracted from dignity and spiritual atmosphere of divine worship. Furthermore, lack of suitable and attractive places of worship was a reproach and source of embarrassment to the Christians themselves. Muslims had their beautiful mosques; Hindus had their intricately carved temples; but Christians had no building at all. "What's wrong with your religion?" asked the non-Christians. "Don't you care enough about your God to erect a house of worship in His name?"

Then it was that Arnett Seamands, the engineer, came to the foreground. His university training in civil engineering was the very skill required at this juncture in the growth of Methodism in south India. Congregations needed places of worship. They needed someone to draw plans, supervise construction, and give general guidance to the building program. It became clear that Arnett was God's engineer to help Christian congregations build their churches.

In December, 1939, Arnett laid the foundation for the first village church, in Tumkur village, Yadgiri District. This particular village was chosen because it was the center of a large and enthusiastic congregation, which was willing to do its share in raising necessary funds. Almost two years later, in August, 1941, the new church was dedicated by their Indian bishop, Bishop S.K. Mondol, amidst great rejoicing and festivity. Because of Arnett's long enforced furlough during World War II, it was not until April, 1944, that the second church building was completed, in the strategic village of Yellari. This was followed by a third sanctuary in the nearby village of Kelebelegundi. By this time other rural congregations were becoming enthusiastic about plans for their places of worship, and thus the whole church-building program was gaining momentum.

The method adapted by the South India Conference for constructing these village churches was both wise and practical. New Christians all came out of the lower castes of Hindu society, so-called "outcaste people" or "untouchables." As such, they were extremely poor, landless, and illiterate, suffering from a lack of self-esteem. They did not possess the financial resources to erect their own church buildings. In fact, they were unable to support their own pastors. Furthermore, these people could not go to a bank and borrow money for their building projects, for they had no collateral to put up for such a loan.

Faced with this situation, mission leaders were sorely tempted to construct the needed sanctuaries with funds received from America, and to make the church buildings an out-and-out gift to poor rural congregations. In fact, in some other areas of Methodism in India, this very policy had been tried. The missionary would choose a strategic village, build a church with mission funds, and then say to the people, "Here's the church, it's our gift to you."

However, missionaries soon began to witness the ill effects of this approach. Christians looked upon these church buildings as mission property, not their own. Later when the buildings needed some repairs—a new coat of whitewash, or new roofing tiles—the congregations refused to do anything about it. When the missionary asked, "Why don't you repair your church?" the people would answer, "It's your church; you repair it." Furthermore, after the first church had been built in an area and given as a gift, other congregations came to the missionaries and said, "When are you going to build a church for us?"

To avoid all these problems, leaders of South India Conference decided on a different plan. Construction of a new church building should be a cooperative agreement. Only after a congregation had done all it could in accordance with its existing resources, would the mission step in and offer assistance. First of all, initiative for a new sanctuary must come from the people themselves. They must sincerely desire to have a church building and be willing to do their part. Each congregation was challenged to give the necessary plot of ground (*bhu-dan*—gift of land), *sampat-dan*—(gift of money), and to pledge a certain amount of free time in hauling materials and doing the unskilled labor (*shrama-dan*—gift of work).

When conference leaders were convinced that a local congregation was doing all it could up to the maximum of its ability, they sought help from donors in the United States to make up the lack in finances and complete the project. In this way, members of local congregations had satisfaction in knowing that they had put their own sweat and tears into building their churches, while at the same time it gave an opportunity for Christian friends in America to reach forth a helping hand.

In all this planning, Arnett's role as engineer was most significant. He went from village to village, challenging congregations to do their part, helping them pick out a suitable plot of ground, and decide on the most practical plan of structure. Then he drew the actual blueprints for the sanctuary and computed the amount of materials needed for the project. During construction of the building he also made several visits, inspecting and supervising work. In this way he gave invaluable technical advice and assistance to the whole building program.

Not only did he give advice, he "got his hands dirty" working with them. Among high caste people, the idea of working with their hands was extremely distasteful and many would not do it. They thought it beneath them. Concerning this, Arnett writes:

> The manual labor of my co-op days has been a double blessing. I learned to really love hard physical work. I set the example in India and insisted that everybody must work with their hands "like Father." If not—they were out!
>
> Also the manual labor added to my physical ruggedness and good health for a long life and service. It was the perfect con-

tinuation to my athletic life in high school and adventurous camping and trekking over Tucson's 10,000 foot Catalina Mountains. Moreover, invaluable to me were the lessons I learned from association with the humble, working man. In India I championed the humblest of the people—the outcastes.

A New Spirit of Sacrifice

As the church building scheme gained momentum it took on every aspect of a spiritual movement. Interest and enthusiasm spread like wildfire throughout the districts. A new spirit of stewardship and self-denial developed among village Christians. At times their demonstrations of sacrifice staggered all of us.

A new spirit of unity also developed among members as each congregation worked toward the common goal of their building project. Furthermore, in each case a completed sanctuary did wonders for the spiritual life of a congregation. It made for better attendance at regular services of the church and for a greater spirit of worship. It afforded a place for revival meetings to be held. It increased offerings and degree of self-support, and also the number of Christian marriage ceremonies. And last, but not least, a church building provided an aspect of permanency to the Christian movement in villages. Now it was clear to non-Christians that Christianity had come to stay.

As a sample of the church-building contagion that continued to sweep the area, we cite one or two illustrations from the villages of Bidar District, the scene of Arnett's pioneer days as a missionary in India. In the fall of 1946, the mantle of the father passed on to his younger son, David, who was superintendent of Bidar District for several years. Stories of self sacrifice that came from this district sound like chapters from the Book of Acts.

During a series of communal riots in 1948, every Christian home in Amalapur village was destroyed by fire. When the Christians of Bidar central church heard about the tragedy, they got together and enacted a Christian drama and raised

300 rupees (Rs. 300) to help the fifteen families rebuild their homes. But the people returned the money saying, "Keep it for us, and when we get back on our feet again, we want to build a church. Give the money to us then, and it will help us buy stones for the building. Never mind about our homes; we will rebuild them somehow, but first we must think about our church!" Two years later, amidst great celebration, Amalapur Church was dedicated.

In Merjapur village, the people had raised their share of finances and free labor, but had not been successful in finding a plot of land for their church. Finally, one of the village elders, Lalappa, stepped forward and offered the plot on which his own home stood. "Tear down my house and build the church in its place," he said.

David and the members of the congregation were completely swept off their feet. They had never before witnessed a spirit of self-denial equal to this. Other villagers soon caught the spirit. The lay leader asked everyone if he would be willing to help build another house for Lalappa on a nearby plot of ground, too small for the church. They gladly agreed, and the very next day started tearing down Lalappa's house. Three days later they were building him a new house, and at the same time laid the cornerstone for the church. Six weeks later David dedicated a beautiful new red stone church! It was a record all the way around.

From 1950 to 1955, David witnessed the construction of approximately thirty-six village churches in his district alone. To describe the situation in his own words, it was "a glorious epidemic!"

The same movement was taking place, on a smaller scale in the western section of South India Conference, where J.T. was serving as superintendent of the Belgaum and Gokak Districts. Between 1947 and 1958 several new churches for rural congregations were constructed in this area under his supervision.

Meanwhile a similar spirit of enthusiasm was taking hold of the larger central congregations in various district headquarters of the conference area. Most of these city congregations were still worshiping in some crowded school hall. They became anxious to possess adequate places. Once again, Arnett, the engineer, was called upon for necessary advice and technical assistance.

In these cases his aid was all the more important, for city congregations required larger and more elaborate church buildings, to command the respect of city residents and to fit in with the architectural environment. A simple and inexpensive style of the village church would not be adequate for a city situation. So Arnett went to work on new plans and new styles.

The first of these city churches was dedicated by Bishop S.K. Mondol at the opening of Annual Conference held in Belgaum, in January, 1948. All conference members were present for this historic event. It was a few years before the next central church was completed, then the program picked up speed. In January, 1956, the beautiful new church at Yadgiri was dedicated. The following year, Raichur central church was completed, and then in December, 1960, Gulbarga central church was opened for worship.

Mention must be made of the unique architectural style that Arnett developed for the Yadgiri and Gulbarga sanctuaries. The style is the same in each case, except that the latter is larger by far, and therefore most impressive of the two buildings. It is built of solid granite, can accommodate about a thousand people, and cost only $14,000.

This architectural design was Arnett's attempt to steer away from the traditional Western style and to adopt a design that is more indigenous to India's culture. All too often Christianity has been severely criticized by non-Christians in India as being too Western and too foreign in all its outward appearances. Missionaries have often been accused of "deculturizing" Indian Christians. So Arnett sought for a typical Indian style of architecture.

From the Muslim style he used picturesque small domes or cupolas on the roof; while from Hindu architecture he used the typical porch that runs along three sides of the building, and twin spindle-like pillars interspersed every few yards on the porch. The distinctive Christian features are the cruciform shape of the entire building, the cross on top, and an unusual paneled front door, which, when opened, also forms the shape of a cross. This design has become the talk of the town and has attracted people from all around. Even non-Christians stand in amazement before the church and exclaim, "This is truly Indian; this is our style; this is beautiful!"

By the time Arnett retired from active service in India during April, 1957, there were about seventy village and city church buildings in the South India Conference. However, this proved to be just the beginning of the program, for Arnett was destined to build many more churches in the next twenty-six years of his "retirement years." Instead of building bridges of steel in America, as he had dreamed of in his youth, he built bridges of love between the church in America and the people of his adopted land of India.

Arnett was not only interested in building attractive churches for Christians to worship in, he was also concerned about providing adequate housing for pastors who shepherded these congregations. His heart was deeply grieved over the terrible living conditions of most of the village pastors. They were living in despicable mud huts with dirt floors, and thatched roofs that leaked in the monsoon season. So whenever he made plans for a new church building, he also made sure that the plot was large enough to construct a parsonage right next to the sanctuary. Over the past forty years he has built almost as many parsonages as he has built churches. Scores of village and city pastors in the South India Conference will long remember Arnett for taking them out of mud huts and putting them into decent homes.

A New Friend

Through the building program Arnett developed a close and beautiful friendship with a very special person in India. In the early 1950s, while Arnett was stationed in Gulbarga, a young Parsee couple, Homi and Pilloo Irani, took up residence in the city. Homi had just returned from the United States where he had obtained a degree in Civil Engineering from Stanford University in California, preparing to become a building contractor.

The Parsees are a remarkable minority community in India, with a long history. By religion they are Zoroastrians, original faith of ancient Persia (now Iran). Their ancestors, seeking religious freedom from Muslim invaders, fled to India in the latter part of the 7th century. Most Parsees live in and around Bombay on the west coast. They are an intelligent, well-educated and advanced community, noted for their business acumen and their generosity to public charity.

At the time of Homi Irani's arrival in Gulbarga, South India Conference was making plans to construct a modern, well-equipped hospital in Yadgiri. Since the funds were being donated by Methodist churches of the Holston Conference in Tennessee, the new center was to be named The Holston Hospital. Arnett immediately recognized unusual qualities in this young graduate from Stanford and recommended him as contractor for the new buildings. It was a wise choice indeed. In Arnett's own words, "Homi proved most proficient as to quality and speed in his work—true American style."

In December, 1955, The Holston Hospital was dedicated amidst much fanfare, while members of South India Conference were convened in Yadgiri for their annual meeting.

The new hospital was Homi Irani's first major building contract. Soon his fame spread through the area, especially in Gulbarga, which was experiencing a building boom at that time. In the last twenty-five years or so, Homi has received the contract for almost every major building project in the city. He has put up private houses, dormitories, schools, and entire college complexes. Today he is one of the most celebrated citizens of Gulbarga.

In the same way Homi Irani became indispensable to the building program of South India Conference. Following Arnett's architectural designs, he built several strategic central churches, including the one in Yadgiri (to seat 500), in Gulbarga (to seat 1,000), and in Bidar (to seat 1,500). Whenever there was an addition made to Holston Hospital, Homi insisted that he be given the contract at minimum cost. He personally donated several private wards and a social center as memorials to some of his family members. In addition he built two schools, a college hostel, and two high school dormitories for the Methodist Church.

Homi had complete confidence in, and a great love for Arnett. Whenever Arnett had a building project under way, Homi would take time to supervise the construction work, no matter how busy he was at the time. Furthermore, realizing how long it sometimes takes to raise the needed funds in U.S.A., instead of building piece-meal as the money came in, Homi would go ahead and finish the project, and then wait patiently for the mission to pay him the full amount—interest free.

After Arnett retired from the field in 1957, Homi and Pilloo Irani made a trip to the States and visited him in his home in Wilmore, Kentucky. Whenever Arnett made his annual trips to India, he would go to Gulbarga and spend several days in the Irani home. Homi kept his car and chauffeur available to Arnett whenever he needed to visit any nearby mission stations. Arnett loved Homi and Pilloo like his own family, and no visit to India was complete without seeing them. Regarding Homi's sacrificial spirit, Arnett wrote:

> When a national of India, a Christian, gives generously to Christ's cause, it is a big thrill indeed. But when a national of a different faith gives lavishly of time, money, and buildings to meet urgent needs in Christ's Kingdom, it is a thrill unique!

6

FOURTH AND FIFTH TERMS

When Arnett and Yvonne returned to India in July, 1944, they were appointed to Gulbarga, where they resided for the rest of their missionary career—until March, 1957—except for a furlough period from January, 1951 to June, 1952. Half the time Arnett served as superintendent of Gulbarga District, and the other half as district missionary. He also had responsibilities as evangelist in the Raichur and Yadgiri Districts.

During this period Arnett was instrumental in leading Gulbarga District forward on several different fronts. First was the annexation of the Kanarese/Telegu-speaking area of Sholapur City, about fifty miles northwest of Gulbarga, on the main railway line to Bombay. An urgent appeal from the American Marathi Mission and the United Church of North India came to the Methodist Church in June, 1947. They requested that the Methodist Church take over their Sholapur Kanarese/Telegu congregations. The Methodist Church agreed and commenced work among the 80,000 people who spoke these languages in this rapidly-growing industrial city. Arnett recognized the tremendous challenge that faced this district, for here within the bounds of one city were as many

Kanarese-and Telegu-speaking people as resided in one hundred average-sized villages in rural areas. Over the years Arnett endeared himself to the Sholapur Christians, for he spent much time in holding revivals in their midst and giving guidance in their plans for buildings and evangelistic outreach. During his lifetime Arnett saw the membership of this congregation increase from 500 to over 2,000, to become the second largest church in South India Conference, next to Bidar Central Church.

The second major advance was southward from Chittapur into an area unoccupied by any church. In the summer of 1946, Arnett organized an intensive evangelistic campaign under the direction of Rev. H.G. Mitra and a team of laymen from Bhimanhalli village. As a result, the majority of people from the *keris* (low caste sections) of three different villages were converted and formed into new congregations with a pastor. This started a movement in a cluster of villages nearby, and today Chittapur Circuit is a flourishing center with a membership of several hundred.

A further outreach was northward toward Chidaguppa, an area also unoccupied by any church, lying between Gulbarga District and Bidar District. Rev. H.G. Mitra and Arnett made an extensive tour of this section, contacting key individuals and sounding out the people's attitude. They received a very warm welcome in the strategic town of Ratkal, and preached for several hours in one of the large shops. Ratkal, they decided, would provide a good center from which to reach into surrounding villages. Progress was slow for several years, and after Arnett's retirement from the field, there was a tendency on the part of the conference to neglect this strategic area. Arnett, however, kept prodding the conference to take the challenge seriously, until finally a good-sized congregation was established in Ratkal. At the time of Arnett's death he was busily drawing plans and raising funds for an adequate and attractive church/parsonage in this town.

Perhaps the greatest advance during this period was in the area of self-support. For ten years Arnett had been seeking to raise the level of stewardship among Christian congregations and to challenge them to increasingly assume responsibility for the support of their pastors. Some progress was made, but it was slow and painful. It was clear that a more drastic approach was necessary. Fortunately, a series of events brought the issue to a crisis.

In 1949 the Communist Party seized power in China and turned the country into a Marxist Republic. Within a year or two the new regime had forced all Christian missionaries to withdraw, and had cut off all foreign funds from Chinese churches. Because mission societies had not developed any system of self-support for Chinese congregations, the sudden denial of financial assistance from abroad proved to be a traumatic experience for Chinese Christians. When missionaries in South India Conference saw this, they decided it would be wise to prepare the Indian Church for any such eventuality. Furthermore, by this time, they were convinced that the continued dependence on foreign subsidy all these years had robbed the Indian Church of a true sense of stewardship and responsibility. It had prevented the Church from "growing up" into maturity. So Arnett, J.T., and David began to stress the importance and urgency of self-support for all national pastors and evangelists. David wrote an especially significant and challenging paper on the biblical principles of tithing and stewardship, pointing out that self-support was not merely financial expediency, but an absolute necessity for spiritual vitality and growth.

At first the Indian brethren reacted with violent opposition. They even suggested that if missionaries were not willing to share American money with the Indian Church to support its pastors, then perhaps it was time for them to withdraw. Tension between national and missionary was high. But fortunately, good sense and Christlike graces prevailed, and soon Indian members of the conference began to lead in the drive for self-support. In December, 1952, South India Annual Conference adopted a Fifteen-Year Plan for Self-Support, whereby each year the mission would cut its subsidy by one-fifteenth, and the church would increase its giving by an equal amount. Thus, by 1967 salaries of all Indian pastors, superintendents, and evangelists (both men and women) would be paid from funds raised in India. Arnett's dream had finally come true!

The 1952 session of the South India Annual Conference was also significant for another historical event.

From Tomb to Palace*

It was only four miles, but it took sixty-eight long years to get there, and the man who began the journey never lived to see it completed.

In 1884, the Rev. S. P. Jacob and his wife had arrived in the historic city of Gulbarga, which at one time had been the capital of the Muslim Bahmani Kingdom. The Jacobs were the first missionaries of The Methodist Church to that section of the country. To people in Gulbarga, Mr. Jacob was a strange man, with a strange face and a strange religion, so no one was willing to rent him a place to live in the city.

About two-and-a-half miles outside Gulbarga City limits, there stands, all alone on a hilltop, a large stone structure, square-shaped with a huge dome. This had been built by a very rich Muslim merchant of the city, and was intended to become the tomb of a famous Muslim saint. But since the merchant had dishonestly acquired most of his wealth, the "saint" refused to grant permission for his body to be buried in the intended tomb. Later, upon his death, he was actually buried in a now-famous mosque in Gulbarga.

The mausoleum, popularly known as the *Chor Gumaz* (Thieves' Tomb), was left standing unused. Being the highest spot for miles around, it can be seen from the city. Mr. Jacob learned that it was unoccupied, and since he and his wife needed a place to stay, they decided to move in. They took their belongings to the top of the hill in bullock carts, and Mrs. Jacob, like any housewife, stood in the middle of the 50 x 55 ft. square, one-room tomb and decided which corner should be the living room. It really didn't matter, since all corners were practically the same. There wasn't even any problem of where to hang clothes in the rainy season. A very high balcony, reaching completely around the top of the room about forty feet up, provided the answer. It was a whispering balcony. Even a whisper on one side could be heard perfectly on the other side. Mrs. Jacob simply draped her skirts, shirts, sheets, and socks over the balcony railing when it was raining.

Of course there were problems. Snakes and scorpions and other dangerous creatures sought the coolness of the stone tomb, and sometimes rats would chew the strings which held up their mosquito nets. But all in all, it wasn't a bad place to live. The Jacobs had no rent to pay and nobody disturbed them.

Daily they made visits into the city, talking to people in the bazaar, in shops, and in their homes, telling the good news of Christ to any who were willing to listen. Mr. Jacob also made a few trips to the surrounding villages, spreading the good news. On one occasion he went as far as Bidar, about seventy-five miles away, and preached for several hours in the bazaar. But the people so threatened his life that he had to escape into darkness.

For nine months the Jacobs lived in their tomb, and many times they stood at the door on the hilltop, watching the sun set in long, streaked, dusty fingers over the city, and prayed that one day Christ would be honored in the midst of the hot, dirty streets below.

One night the Jacobs were awakened by heavy footsteps, loud talking, and their doors being forced open. A robber gang that had been away on extended exploits had returned to their old hideout—the tomb—only to find it occupied by foreigners. The Jacobs were forced to run for their lives, leaving everything they owned to the gang of thieves. They fled to Hyderabad, where they gave two years of devoted service before returning to the United States.

Then came the first ray of light amidst the darkness.

In November, 1888, a high-caste Hindu came to Rev. J.H.

Garden, another missionary who, by this time, had been able to build a house in Gulbarga. The Hindu man declared his faith in Jesus Christ, and asked Rev. Garden for Christian baptism. He had heard the good news preached during a Hindu jathra in Tinthani, a small village about twenty-five miles out from Gulbarga. This man, Bachanna, and his family were baptized and became the first Methodist converts in the Nizam's Dominions. At last the seed of the Gospel was taking root in the soil! It was a small beginning, but though the Church may begin small, it always grows.

By 1952 there were approximately 56,000 Kanarese-speaking Christians in the Raichur-Gulbarga-Bidar area. In Gulbarga itself there was a thriving congregation of 600 members, and a coeducational high school with more than 1,000 students. The mission compound, where the congregation met for regular worship, was located in the very heart of the city. Three grandsons of Bachanna, that first convert, were serving in the conference: two had their M.A. degrees and were engaged in educational work, one was an ordained minister who later became a district superintendent.

In 1952, South India Annual Conference was to convene in the city of Gulbarga where Dad was superintendent. Dad realized there would not be enough room to house all ministerial and lay delegates of the conference in bungalows on the mission compound. So Dad requested the new state government of Hyderabad to permit the conference to use the Nizam's summer palace, which was right next door. The palace was beautiful and spacious, with a well-kept garden all around. It was used only rarely, when His Highness the Nizam would visit; at other times it was closed.

The state government granted Dad's request, so Methodists took over the palace for a week. Bishop S.K. Mondol occupied the royal suite of the Nizam. Cabinet meetings were held in the magnificent reception room. Ladies of the Woman's Society of Christian Service found it hard to concentrate on their business at hand, for in luxury they were reclining on soft sofas and satin pillows, and peering around silken curtains in rooms where the Nizam's harem used to play.

Thus, in the period of sixty-eight years, the Gospel had gone from outside the city limits to the very center of the city. It had jumped from tomb to palace! All those years God had been taking people out of the tombs—people who were dead in trespasses and sins—and had been transforming them into sons and daughters of the King of Kings!

If the Jacobs could visit their old hilltop tonight they would see the ancient tomb still dark and deserted. But their hearts would be glad, for they could hear the Christians singing below, and they could see the Cross of Christ glowing on Gulbarga Church in the heart of the dusty city.

*by J.T. Seamands. Originally printed in the *World Outlook*, December, 1960. Used with permission.

7

ACTIVE RETIREMENT

Mother and Dad retired from the field in April, 1957, having served in India for over thirty-seven years. (Dad was sixty-five years old, and Mother, 63 at the time.) They took up residence in Wilmore, Kentucky, where they built a two-bedroom home.

But Dad never intended his retirement to be the termination of his missionary career; for him, it was merely a change in residence, a change in direction. The next twenty-seven years were destined to be one of the most fruitful periods of his whole life. In one of his patron letters Dad wrote:

Retirement *in* and *for Christ* is glorious and deeply satisfying!

God gave me my goal in 1951, seven years before retirement. It was during our last furlough as we listened on the radio to General Douglas McArthur's masterful farewell address before the American Congress. Rising to a grand finale, he quoted the well-known military slogan, "Old soldiers never die, they just fade away!" The Holy Spirit whispered, *"That's not for you!* As an old soldier of the cross, don't you just *fade away*; you keep on *firing away!"* I responded, "Lord, that's a deal. I will, provided you inspire the saints to bring up the ammunition!"

Once an elderly visitor came to Wilmore, and on meeting Dad, gave him his card. On the front side, in the middle, was the man's name; then in the four corners there appeared: "No phone – no address – no money – no business." On the back of the card was a little poem about the man's daily routine. On waking he would grab the morning newspaper and look over the list of obituaries. If his name was not there, then he knew he was not dead; so he would enjoy a good breakfast, and go back to bed.

Dad remarked, "That's not the life for me! When I retired, the Heavenly Father speedily refreshed, refilled, refired and rehired me. The Calendar and *Discipline* say 'retire,' but Christ says, 'Be faithful even unto death'!"

Earl Meets Merle

For the first few years of his "active retirement," Dad traveled extensively in the States, conducting mission conferences in various Methodist churches and raising funds for his church-building program in India.

On one of these occasions—Sunday, March 2, 1958—Dad was speaking at the final service of a week-long mission conference being conducted at Wesley Methodist Church in Wesleyville, Pennsylvania. Just before the opening hymn, he noticed a man being wheeled in upon a reclining chair. The chair was brought right up to the front of the sanctuary, just to the left of the pulpit. At a glance, Dad could see that the man was a helpless invalid, completely paralyzed except for his hands and arms. But there was a radiance on his face, and an interest that attracted Dad's attention.

After finishing his missionary address, Dad stepped down from the platform and went over to the man in the wheelchair. He put out his hand and said, "I am Rev. Seamands from India. I am happy to meet you, my brother." The invalid extended his hand and responded, "I am Merle Cook, and it's a joy to meet you, too."

There was something providential about that handshake that morning. It was destined to be the inauguration of an

amazing new partnership for Christ which would bring together the needs of a congregation and the longings of a
man, separated by ten thousand miles.

In his youth Merle Cook had been active in athletics and
in church work, but when he was seventeen years of age, a
freak accident injured his spine and left him completely paralyzed, except for his hands and arms. The next fifteen years
was a period of suffering and struggle for Merle, both phy-
sically and spiritually. He became withdrawn and bitter toward life.

One day a group of young people came into his bedroom,
sang Gospel songs and witnessed to him. In desperation
Merle cried out to the Lord for help. And so at the age of
thirty-two, he became a new person in Christ and began to
really live for the first time in his life. He began to study
God's Word and to go to church regularly in his specially-
built, reclining wheelchair.

That Sunday morning when they shook hands, Merle Cook
said to Dad, "Brother Seamands, oh how I would love to do
something for India; but look at me, what can I do?"

In desperation, Dad said, "Brother Cook, let's pray about
it, shall we?" During the prayer, the Holy Spirit whispered
to Dad, "Tell him the story of Lizzie Johnson."

Then Dad began to briefly narrate the story of that amazing saint of God from Casey, Illinois. At the age of thirteen
she was smitten with a mysterious disease of the spine that
left her an invalid, flat on her back, for the greater part of
the next twenty-seven years of her life. But she surrendered
her life to God and to the cause of Christian missions, and by
embroidering a "crazy quilt" and making ribbon bookmarks,
she was able to send thousands of dollars across seas. She
supported village pastors and school children, and even built
a great church in one of the cities of India.

The word "embroider" supplied the key! Merle's mother,
who stood by the wheelchair and heard the story, suddenly
exclaimed with joy, "Brother Seamands, Merle does that.
Merle embroiders!"

Merle himself was quick to see the open door. "Brother Seamands," he said, "I'll embroider a tablecloth for you. If you can use it for God's glory in India, I'll be ever so happy."

It just so happened that Merle had already embroidered a beautiful linen tablecloth with a butterfly design for his sister-in-law, Caroline. When she heard of Merle's plan for missions, she immediately returned the tablecloth so that it might be used for the project. Two weeks later, at a special Sunday morning service, the tablecloth was dedicated at Wesley Methodist Church in Wesleyville by Dr. Albert Merriott, then superintendent of the Erie District. Members of the congregation came forward and placed a cash offering of approximately $400 on the cloth. During the next few months they increased the amount to almost $2,500.

The tablecloth was then sent to my father, who took it along on his missionary meetings, and told the story of Merle Cook and his dedication to Christ. Then he challenged those who were in sympathy with Merle's project to place their offerings on the cloth. In this way, the total amount raised came to $11,000! Dad used this money for constructing the beautiful Christ Methodist Church in Gulbarga, scene of the story "From Tomb to Palace."

After this, Merle Cook began to embroider bookmarks for sale, and with the proceeds two more churches were later erected in Gulbarga District—in Chittapur and Kachapur.

Shuttle Service Missions

In the fall of 1958, Dad began to make annual work tours to India, or what he called his "shuttle service missions." He usually went for a period of three months at a time. The objectives of these "missions" were to:

1. Renew fellowship with pastors and lay people of South India Conference.

2. Hold evangelistic meetings and keep the fire of evangelism burning within the conference.

3. Attend Dharur Jathra.

4. Survey the needs for new churches and parsonages.

During each mission Dad would travel the entire length and breadth of the conference, holding to a very rigid schedule that he had prepared far in advance. He witnessed and preached wherever he went. Each year he either laid the cornerstone for, or dedicated several new churches, for which he had raised funds and drawn blueprints. He also received petitions for help on new sanctuaries from several other rural congregations. These would provide his "homework" upon his return to the States, until his next mission the following year.

In his first mission, in 1958, Dad visited all the major centers, from Sholapur in the north to Bangalore in the south, and Belgaum in the west. At the Executive Committee of the Conference, which convened in January, the members passed a unanimous resolution, stating that Dad's visit "was of such great spiritual and technical help, that he should be invited to return to India annually for such services, until South India Conference was able to find a resident engineer to take his place."

Between 1958 and 1965, Dad made eight consecutive "shuttle service missions." While at home in Kentucky he traveled extensively in deputation work, raising money and drawing plans for his building projects. Then on his trips to India he witnessed the completion of these projects and at the same time surveyed areas for new projects.

On his second mission to India in the fall of 1959, Dad had the great joy of holding the first service in the newly-built Christ Methodist Church in Gulbarga, where he had served for so many years. He told the congregation of Merle Cook and his painful work to help make this church possible. After the dedication many non-Christians came from all around just to see the unusual style of the new church, which incorporated architecture from Hindu, Muslim, and Christian religious buildings.

On the third mission, Mother went along with Dad and spent most of the time with David and Helen, who were then serving in the Richmond Town Methodist Church in Bangalore. Dad toured for six weeks over the whole Conference, laying plans for sixteen new church buildings. He preached in Dharur Jathra and in the Golden Jubilee Session of the Holiness Convention at Yeotmal. During his term in India he had served as president of the India Holiness Association for several years, and had given significant leadership to this organization. He always paid travel expenses of several Indian pastors and superintendents to the convention each year, so they would be exposed to the biblical doctrine of holiness.

Immediately upon his return from the fourth mission in January, 1962, Dad had to undergo surgery for a cataract in his left eye. He was limited for four months and had to cancel all his speaking engagements. But by fall he was on his way back to India for the fifth time. During the flight out, however, Dad felt a strange sensation in his left eye, so when he arrived in India he went to Holston Hospital in Yadgiri. He went to Dr. Raleigh Pickard who had just opened a new eye ward in the hospital. The doctor discovered that Dad had a detached retina in his left eye and urged him to return to the United States immediately for corrective surgery. Commenting on this sudden turn of events, sometime later Dad wrote in a letter to his donors:

Wow! Just to think—I had to come all the way from old Kentucky to be the first "star patient" in the new Eye Ward. Mission No. 5 had suddenly struck a road block! Lying in bed I closed my eyes to see all my plans in panorama disappearing down the Indian Road.

The next three months was an exciting battle for sight. God was deepening my love and sympathy for India's and the world's innumerable eye-sufferers.

Dad was admitted to the famous Eye Institute of the Presbyterian Hospital in New York, where he underwent two operations to try to save the sight in his left eye. However, the long flight to India and back, rough travel by taxi and train in India itself, and the consequential delay in treatment, all combined to prevent successful surgery. Dad lost sight in his left eye. He had to give up driving a car and this considerably curtailed his deputation work in the United States.

During his twenty-three-day stay in the Presbyterian Hospital, Dad witnessed to, and prayed with, many of the patients. He also witnessed to the nurses and doctors. His own surgeon, Dr. Graham Clark, proved to be a committed Christian and he and Dad developed a close friendship.

In the fall of 1963, when Dad was contemplating his sixth "shuttle service mission" to India, he wrote to Dr. Clark asking his advice on whether he should go. Dr. Clark wrote:

> As to whether it would be "safe" for you to carry out another part of your mission to India, I don't recall Jesus ever telling the disciples to play it safe. No, your earthly safety is not at stake, and their need of you would make it unsafe for you not to go. (Letter dated Aug. 6, 1963.)

On Mission No. 6, in the fall of 1963, Dad broke ground for one new church, laid the cornerstone for ten churches under construction, dedicated five completed sanctuaries, and laid plans to build twenty-five more.   His age, 72.

Regarding Mission No. 7 Dad wrote:

> We pushed ahead our Church Extension Program with vim and vigor on this mission, dedicating ten new churches and launching plans for eighteen more churches and direly needed parsonages. These figures are more than cold statistics. In life they mean that some 4,000 Methodist Christians over South India ceased worshiping their Savior out of doors or in huts, and for the first time in their lives held their Christmas services indoors in lovely new churches of their own.

Highlight of Mission No. 7 was the dedication of the New St. Paul's Methodist Church in Bidar, where Dad had served as superintendent from 1922 to 1925. This is, without doubt, his masterpiece. It is a most impressive building, in the shape of a cross, with twin towers and domes in front, a series of twin pillars on both side-verandas, scallops all along the roofing (to match the famous old Bidar fort just across the street), and a beautiful stained glass cross window behind the pulpit. The church seats 1,500 and was constructed at a cost of $25,000. Of this amount the congregation itself raised $10,000 (a record in the conference), and St. Paul's Methodist Church in Louisville, Kentucky, contributed the balance.

Rev. Henry Lacy, India Secretary in the Division of World Missions in New York at that time, declared that it was a record in the history of Methodism for ten new churches to be dedicated within a twenty-day period.

During one of these church dedication programs, a nearby village sent a delegation of fifteen men, demanding that Dad come to their village and baptize several hundred people who had surrendered themselves to Christ.

Another feature of Mission No. 7 was the large number of young people who responded to a call to the ministry under Dad's preaching. About this, Dad wrote:

> I fished for recruits for Christ's ministry and saw seventeen more fine high school lads added to the list. Now there are twenty-five. Praise the Lord!

Being a very practical person, Dad could see the financial implications of so many recruits for the Christian ministry, so he started an endowment fund to help provide tuition scholarships for ministerial candidates in seminary. The first substantial contribution to this fund ($840.00) was made by Dad's good friend, Homi Irani, the Parsee contractor. Another close friend, Mr. Wane Zimmerman of Tucson, Arizona, also contributed generously to the project. Today the Seamands Scholarship Fund stands at Rupees 150,000, and tuition is guaranteed for every young person who desires to go to seminary.

Mission No. 8 in the fall of 1965 was significant because of the Diamond Jubilee celebration of the beginning of the Methodist work in the Hyderabad area. Members of South India Annual Conference convened in Gulbarga to celebrate the 80th anniversary of the coming of Rev. and Mrs. S.P. Jacob to that city. Once again the pageant of "From Tomb to Palace" was reenacted, but this time the picture was complete, for the beautiful new Christ Methodist Church was standing right in the heart of the city, next to the summer palace of the former Nizam of Hyderabad. An excerpt from the 1965 South India Conference Minutes reads:

> What a thrilling procession it was! At least three-quarters of a mile long, it included over 2,500 members of the Christian community. In front of the town band rode the organizer of the celebration, the Rev. H. G. Mitra, mounted on a handsomely decorated, chestnut- colored stallion. Behind him came eight camels, ridden by some of the more adventuresome young men of the conference. Then came people on foot—nearly a thousand of them—followed by a procession of 93 bullock carts, 30 tongas (two-wheeled, horse-drawn vehicles), and 14 jeeps, all bursting with men, women, and children in gay holiday attire, while an uncounted number of cyclists wove their way in and out of the throngs. Everyone was singing and waving his paper flag, which displayed a cross, flanked by the *Chor Gumaz* (Thieves' Tomb) on one side and Christ Church on the other. The gaiety and dignity of this astonishing number of Christians obviously impressed the townspeople, who crowded the bazaars to witness such an unusual sight.

> When the procession reached the Thieves' Tomb, about four miles outside the city, a brief service of commemoration was held. Then all returned to the mission compound for fireworks, pageant and entertainment. The quadrangle of the new Seamands' wing of the Methodist High School accommodated thick-packed rows of spectators. They thoroughly enjoyed the carefully prepared historical pageant, presenting Christian leaders from pioneer days to the present, folk dances beautifully executed by small girls of the boarding school, and songs especially composed for

the occasion. Everyone was particularly delighted with the beautiful painted back-drop for the quadrangle's stage. It depicted the old Tomb in somber tones on the left, while the new Christ Church of Gulbarga gleamed white on the right, with light streaming over it from the Cross in the sky above. This symbolism seemed especially fitting next morning, when the stage became a sanctuary for the Jubilee Thanksgiving and the Communion service for all the people.

And in the final service of this celebration, on the platform with Bishop Sundaram and district superintendents sat our honored guests, including Dr. E. A. Seamands, to whom the occasion was a "mighty dream come true." Greetings and messages were brought by delegates from other conferences and major boards of the Methodist Church in India. Twenty babies and young people were baptized, and forty-five persons received into full membership of the local Christ Church. Seven deacons and four elders were then ordained by the bishop. Following the deeply moving Ordination Service, Bishop Sundaram led the congregation in the Sacrament of the Lord's supper. In solemn silence over 1,250 people partook of the elements at the same moment, knowing communion with God and with each other. With fervor and exaltation thus came to end the unforgettable Diamond Jubilee of the Deccan.

Term of Endearment

It was during the early part of his retirement years that the honorific title *Thatha* was given to Dad. In the Kanarese language of India, "Thatha" means grandfather, but it is more than a word designating blood relationship. It is a word of both endearment and respect, and carries with it the idea of "beloved, honorable grandfather." For thirty years now, no one addressed Dad as "Doctor" or "Reverend" Seamands. In India and the States alike, everyone called him Thatha—family members, friends, church leaders, village Christians, college and seminary students and professors.

Dad accepted the title as a real honor and delighted in being addressed in that manner. He called himself Thatha.

When his Indian friends started calling him that, he wrote to one of the Indian ministers asking: "Why do all the Indian people call me Thatha, when you have not called others by that name?"

In response, Rev. K. Gnany, principal of Bidar High School, wrote the following letter:

> You have put a difficult question for me to answer. Rev. King, Ernsberger, Lipp, Ross, all became old men and yet, why is it that you alone are called "Thatha"?
>
> I have given this matter a little thinking and this is what I feel. These missionaries whom you have mentioned have, no doubt, served faithfully with dedication as pioneers as long as they were in India on active service. The moment they retired—they lost all personal contacts with India and the people among whom they worked. You have not done this. Your shuttle-service program and the intensely personal letters to almost every worker here on the field has endeared you to all of us here. You know so many of us here personally by name. Hence our endearing term for you, "Thatha." For us it does not so much denote age, it denotes love, respect, almost veneration. The young Hindus touch the feet of their parents, grandparents, and elders, as a mark of respect for the sacrificial love of their elders and for their accumulated experience and wisdom. It is probably a little different in the States. It is the "young people's world" over there. You know so many people all over South India by their first name. You know their wives' names, something of their family history and their children. This general personal relationship has endeared you to all of us and we therefore call you Thatha. We do this out of respect, love, gratitude, and veneration. How can the little children, born after you left India, resist loving you and calling you "Thatha" when you yourself sing, "Thatha comes"?

There is humor and deep love behind those lines.

The Growth of Dharur Jathra

One of the significant experiences of each of the eight shuttle Service Missions described thus far was Arnett's attendance at the Dharur Jathra, which takes place annually from Tuesday evening to Sunday noon in the third week of November. Each year Arnett would plan to arrive a week or two before the camp meeting—to recover from jet lag resulting from the long flight out—and then go straight to Dharur. Being one of the founders of the Jathra (1923), his presence and messages were always a tremendous inspiration to the people gathered there. Playing his cymbals, and with a radiant smile, he would join in heartily with the *bhajana* (song service) conducted by the congregation. In his sermons he would emphasize the theme "Tarry Until," and exhort the congregation to enter into their personal experience of Pentecost. As the camp grew in numbers and years rolled on, Arnett was always concerned that the original purpose of the jathra should not be lost in pageantry. He kept holding up before leaders and people the necessity and beauty of the Spirit-filled life.

From year to year the attendance at Dharur Jathra kept increasing. In 1958, when Arnett made his first Shuttle Service Mission to India, the attendance was about 4,000 with an offering of Rupees 1,200. By 1965, when he made his eighth trip, the attendance had gone up to roughly, 8,000; two years later it reached the 10,000 mark, and the offering was about the same figure.

About this time a beautiful relationship developed between two important camp meetings in the States and Dharur Camp meeting in India. The first was with Camp Sychar in Mt. Vernon, Ohio, where Arnett first received his call and was confronted with the claims of Christ. It was only natural that the people of Camp Sychar would be interested in a camp meeting that one of their "sons in the Gospel" had established in far-off India. The other camp was Cherry Run Camp Meeting in Pennsylvania, where Yvonne had attended as a young girl. In 1968, when his two sons were the evangelists at Cherry Run, Arnett re-established contact with the people there, and they took on the Dharur Jathra as their mission project. Regularly both Camp Sychar and Cherry

Run Camp sent several hundred dollars to Arnett each year, to buy tents, a generator and public address system for Dharur Camp in India. It was a beautiful link-up between the home front and the field.

Arnett also developed an endowment fund to help pay travel expenses of all village pastors in South India Conference, who desired to attend Dharur Jathra. He wanted them to benefit from the spiritual impact of the meetings, and he knew that on their meager salaries many of them would not be able to attend. This fund today stands at Rupees 150,000, and is drawing 10% interest annually. The village pastors have been most grateful to Arnett for this timely help down through the years.

In the fall of 1971, Arnett made his ninth Shuttle Service Mission to India. He dedicated four new churches and two new parsonages. The Audio-Visual Department of the Methodist Church in India brought their cameras and sound equipment to Dharur and produced a 30-minute, 16mm. film on the history of the camp meeting. Entitled "Streams of Living Water," this color-sound film stars Arnett as one of the founders of Dharur Camp Meeting, and depicts the growth of the Methodist Church in South India and Hyderabad Conferences.

Commentary on the E.A. Seamands Household, 1972

Today I (Ruth) took a loaf of fresh homemade bread and went to visit Dad and Mother Seamands for an afternoon chat. Their retirement home is in Wilmore, just across the street from Asbury College's campus and we live only a block away, so we are often together. When I went in, Mother was all steamed up about something and it seemed I had interrupted a conversation.

"Hi, Mother."

"Oh, come on in, Ruth. Arnett's in there at his desk."

"Everything OK?"

"Oh, that man drives me crazy!"

"Come on, Mother! You know you love him!"

She was feisty. "But he's so peculiar—"

"Now, Mother, you know you love him, even if he does have some peculiarities! Everybody has some."

"Yes, well, everybody calls Arnett a Saint—but in heaven I'm going to get a crown as big as a house for living with him!"

"What's he done now?"

Mother picked up an imaginary piece of dust from the immaculate carpet. "Oh, I get bored with the subject of India morning, noon and night! He can't carry on any conversation for the space of three minutes without bringing in India. If I have company and we want to talk, Arnett goes on and on about India. And as soon as he brings up the subject, his mind hop-scotches over all of India's problems—social, political, and religious. I've *lived* India for fifty-three years now and it's time I had a good rest!"

I laughed. "Yes, I guess so—but I don't think you'll get it."

"And another reason," she stated, "is that he *prowls* through the house all the time. As he talks he simply cannot sit still and relax. He is on his feet, pacing up and down the room, wearing out the carpet, and walking between me and the television! That eternal quest to solve India's problems interferes with me and my television programs!"

"You'd be pretty lonesome if you had the house all to yourself, now wouldn't you?" I asked.

She snapped back, "At least it would be clean!"

I walked back into Dad's office to say hello to him. Looking around I agreed that Mother is going to have a big crown in heaven for living with this mess. And it *is* a total mess to anyone but Dad. Mother is a perfectionist housekeeper and abhors even the tiniest thing out of place, but for all these years she has put up with his *saving* everything. But he knows where things are—most of the time. Mother Seamands used to keep that room as a small dining room and Arnett with his clutter was relegated to the basement. But over the years he filled up the basement with all the paraphernalia he saves. He lived in India long enough to absorb the belief that one isn't supposed to ever throw away anything, so the basement is loaded with his savings.

There are old egg cartons—just like new. Balls of string carefully salvaged from packages; old pairs of shoes he just might need for working in the yard some day; cardboard boxes of all sizes and shapes that don't stack very well; bottles and jars and cans and wooden boxes from India. He saves old wrapping paper; every nail he ever pulled out of an old board; old boots and mis-matched gloves; window panes which wouldn't fit any window anyone ever heard of; suitcases and trunks molded with age; paper sacks—enough to tote food for the starving of India. I knew there were also stubs of pencils and crayons; envelopes full of stamps from exotic countries around the world, in addition to the name and address of every person who ever gave him a dime for missions.

But most of all his papers! Tons of papers! Books and boxes and drawers full of papers—letters from 57 years. His diaries. If you wanted to know, for example, the temperature of April 16, 1921, or where he shot a venison, or how he killed a cobra, or when he had typhus, just ask him. It's all there in his diaries.

The basement filled up, and he had to move somewhere. Mother began to have trouble walking—which, in one way, was good for her because she couldn't go down to the basement and see what a disgrace it was. And I didn't tell her. But Dad said it was too cold for him down there and suggested he had to move upstairs. So they gave us their extra dining room furniture and Dad got some help and moved his groaning old desk upstairs.

Now, today, when I walked in, his office was a repetition of the basement—or beginning to be.

"Dad, would you like for me to help you clean up this office?"

He looked around and answered in his usual slow way, "Oh—I don't think so, Ruth. I'll get to it one of these days. If anybody else moves anything I won't be able to find it the next time I want it—and I'm sure to want it soon as it's moved."

"Dad, this is getting impossible. I can't even see the washer and dryer over there in the corner, you've got so many things piled on top of them. Look at this!" I picked up a paper sack from the Ben Franklin store. Just a little paper sack, but on the front of it he had written, "Bought paper and envelopes July 10, 1969."

"Why are you keeping this?"

He laughed at himself—"I don't know. Just thought I'd keep it!"

I laughed too. "Yes, Dad, you're really one of a kind!" I went over and hugged him.

I knew that when he had moved upstairs with his office work, he really meant to keep it all straight to please Mother, but he just wasn't made that way. Things stack up. But he knows where every *letter* is, no matter if it's from Zachariah Frank Adams, filed under the F's. He remembers the whereabouts of every pile of paper clips, rubber bands, T.V. stamps, every checkbook, slide rule and—most of all—the blueprint for every church he ever built.

I also knew that from this messy office at least ten handwritten letters a day go out. Sometimes he writes just to tell people how much he appreciates them. At times he writes a letter of chastisement if he feels it is called for. He writes to his grandchildren and other relatives—always keeping in touch. But over everything else, his fertile brain is always thinking up contents of brochures and newsletters and reports for hundreds of people in America who are interested in his work in India. For every year he goes on a trip back to India, where his heart really is.

I put my loaf of bread on the kitchen table. I knew they would enjoy it together for supper—while they talked about India! Then I came home and wrote all this down.

New Responsibilities at Home

In the fall of 1973, Dad was back in India for a tenth mission to celebrate the Golden Jubilee (fiftieth anniversary) of the founding of Dharur Camp meeting. Attendance increased to 14,000. During his stay he dedicated ten more churches and two new parsonages.

The next several years proved to be a difficult and trying period for the veteran missionary, but at the same time it helped to bring out some of his most sterling qualities. From 1974 on, Mother's physical condition began to deteriorate. At first she could get around the house with the help of a walker, and then with a wheelchair. But after some time she became confined to a reclining chair. Dad had to hire a part-time nurse to take care of her during the major part of the day, and to prepare the noon meal. He himself helped to dress and undress her, bathe her, see to her toilet needs and prepare breakfast and the evening meal. All of these duties he performed with a degree of patience and devotion which was most exemplary.

Dad's heart was still in India all this time. He longed to continue his annual shuttle-service missions to the field, but he decided that his life's companion must take priority over all other activities for the present. Dad always felt that Mother had made a great sacrifice by leaving behind a comfortable home in the States, going out to India with him, and taking care of his physical welfare all those many years of their missionary career. (Mother had never felt a personal call to the mission field, but as a faithful wife felt that her place was with her husband, wherever God should lead him.) So Dad felt he owed a debt of love to Mother for her many years of loving care.

Dad's home office now became the center of his missionary activities. He spent hours each day writing letters to all his friends, to various pastors, conference leaders, and even bishops. His hand never failed him. Even up to the time of his death at ninety-two years, his handwriting was as firm and legible as ever. He was constantly printing brochures with pictures of the camp meeting and new church buildings, making appeals for funds to build more village churches and parsonages in India. His jacket and overcoat pockets were always stuffed with these folders, and whenever he met anyone on the street he would give the person a sales-talk on missions and hand him a brochure.

During these years, J.T. was teaching at Asbury Theological Seminary and was using his weekends to conduct missionary conferences in a great number of United Methodist churches. In each church he presented the need for erecting church buildings in India, and was instrumental in raising a considerable sum of money for this purpose. Whenever a church or individuals showed interest in taking on a church project, J.T. would put them in touch with Dad, who knew exactly where a church was needed in India and where the congregation had already taken the initiative. Dad would draw the blueprints, send the money out to India and see the project to completion, with full report and pictures.

Meanwhile the home situation became more and more difficult as Mother's condition deteriorated still further. One could see the increasing strain on Dad as he labored heroically to minister to her needs, besides doing much of the cooking, washing and ironing. Then the situation came to a crisis when it was discovered that Dad's heartbeat was very slow and he was in immediate need of a pace-maker. So arrangements were made for the operation. Mother was admitted into Mayfair Manor Nursing Home on Tate's Creek Pike, in Lexington, Kentucky, on May 3, 1978. At first she was bitter over the arrangement and accused her husband and two sons of forsaking her and brutally "committing her to an institution." But in the course of a few months, her attitude completely changed, and she looked upon Mayfair Manor as her own home, and the staff as her loving friends.

Nine days after Mother's admittance into the nursing home, the pace-maker was successfully implanted into Dad's chest.

After he recovered from the operation and for the next few years, Dad's schedule was cut out for him. In the mornings he would work at home in his office in Wilmore, writing letters and brochures, and then each afternoon he would catch a ride into Lexington to visit Mother for a couple of hours. Sometimes J.T. or Ruth, David or Helen would drive him into town (about 17 miles); at times some seminary wife would give him a ride on her way to work. If no one he knew could take him, he stood down at the corner station and hitched a ride. Often then Dr. Dennis Kinlaw, Jr., brought him back to Wilmore after finishing his work in a Lexington hospital. The people of Wilmore were most gracious in providing transportation when he needed it.

In the three years and five months that Mother was bedridden in Mayfair Manor, Dad hardly missed a day in visiting her. By count he made 1,116 trips into Lexington, a total of almost 38,000 miles, the equivalent of one-and-a-half times around the world at the equator. Dad seemed to be courting Mother all over again. He often took her flowers and ice cream. He read to her for long periods. He sang to her the old-time love songs, such as "Let me call you sweetheart," "I love you truly," and "Always." At the end of the visit he would sing some of the old Gospel hymns, especially those which spoke of heaven and life hereafter, and Mother, with her now cracked and weakened voice, would join in with him. Then Dad would hold Mother's hand and offer a prayer for her, and finally kiss her goodbye. On February 22, 1981, they celebrated their 66th wedding anniversary at the Manor, and the Lexington Herald ran an article honoring them. On September 24 of that same year, Mother's brave heart finally gave out and she slipped away peacefully to be with the Lord. She was 87 years of age.

A Very Close Friend

During Dad's years of retirement, a very special and meaningful friendship developed between himself and another outstanding senior citizen of Wilmore, Dr. J.C. McPheeters.

A sort of David-and-Jonathan relationship existed between these two veterans of the Gospel. The two men had much in common both in personality and lifestyle. They were always radiant and joyful, full of laughter and praise. They never spoke a negative word about anyone, but always looked on the bright side of every situation. Evangelism and missions were their chief concern. They both preached sanctification and the Spirit-filled life, and demonstrated the beauty of holiness in their daily lives. Each one remained active long after formal retirement, and was "on the go" for God right up to the end. Dad worked unceasingly and raised money for the church in India; Brother "Mac" did the same for Asbury Theological Seminary, where he had served as President for over twenty years.

Dad had developed a great love and respect for Dr. McPheeters many years before. When Dad's father, John L. Seamands, was living in Tucson and working on the Southern Pacific Railroad as a conductor, Rev. J.C. McPheeters served as pastor of a Methodist Church in the city for several years. It was at this time, through a personal witness of pastor McPheeters, that Grandfather Seamands made a commitment of himself to Jesus Christ. Dad was always grateful to Brother Mac for the spiritual impact that he made on his father, and never ceased to talk about it.

During his extended furlough in the States from early 1942 to mid 1944, Dad and Mother had resided in Wilmore, where Dr. McPheeters was then serving as President of Asbury Theological Seminary. In was in June of 1942 that Dr. McPheeters conferred upon Dad the honorary degree of Doctor of Divinity on behalf of the seminary. The two men became well acquainted at that time, and then after 1957, when Dad retired and settled down in Wilmore, their relationship developed into a deep, life-long friendship.

It was always a special spiritual treat when both men were present at the Friday morning Men's Prayer Breakfast at the Wilmore United Methodist Church. Their spontaneous songs, prayer and witness, lifted all the men to new spiritual heights.

It was a special blessing to watch Dad and Dr. McPheeters unexpectedly meet on the sidewalk or in some store in Wilmore. The occasion always called for a particular ritual. They would place their hands on one another's shoulders, and then with broad smiles burst out singing lustily, "It is joy unspeakable and full of glory," or "The end is not yet, praise the Lord!"

When Dr. McPheeters suffered a severe stroke in April, 1983, and was confined to a convalescent home in Lexington, Dad was deeply moved. He often visited "Brother Mac" and prayed with him, but was grieved that his dear friend was unable to communicate with him.

Just a few days before Dad left on his last trip to India, he paid a final visit to Dr. Mac in the Lexington Country Place, and this turned out to be a memorable occasion. Dr. Mac was in good spirits; his mind quite clear. There was not much verbal communication, but there was a genuine meeting of heart and mind. Dad came away very much encouraged.

A few days later, however, on the very evening that Dad was flying out of New York, Brother McPheeters, at the age of 94, quietly slipped away to be with his Lord. Dad did not receive the news until about ten days later in India. Little did we realize at the time that within a short period of four months Dad himself would join his beloved friend in Heaven.

8

AWARDS AND HONORS

During his thirty-eight years as a missionary in India (1919 - 1957), Dad received only one honor in recognition of distinguished service. While on furlough in June, 1942, Asbury Theological Seminary conferred upon him the honorary degree of Doctor of Divinity. All the other awards were heaped upon him after he was eighty-four years of age. Joking about this, Dad remarked: "How come, a fellow doesn't seem to become DIStinguished until he is almost EXtinguished!?"

Dad's first post-retirement award came in October, 1975, when South India Conference celebrated its Centenary and named him as "The Missionary of the Century." The conference sent him a beautiful bronze plaque with the following inscription:

M.C.S.A.
(Methodist Church of Southern Asia)
Centenary 1876 - 1976
Missionary of the Century Award
Rev. Dr. E. A. Seamands, "Thatha"
Given at the Centenary Celebrations
South India Annual Conference, Madras
October 17, 1975
JAI CHRIST

Congratulations poured in from many quarters. The *Herald-Leader* of Lexington, Kentucky, the *Jessamine Journal* of Nicholasville, Kentucky, the *Arizona Daily Star* of Tucson, Arizona, the Kentucky and Holston *United Methodist Reporters* all carried articles about Dad and the award. *Good News* magazine ran a special feature on his long and distinguished missionary career.

Dad's next award came four-and-a-half years later from his college *alma mater*. Early in 1980 Dad received the following letter from Kirk C. Valanis, Dean of the College of Engineering of the University of Cincinnati:

January 31, 1980

Dear Dr. Seamands:

The faculty of the College of Engineering desires to honor alumni who, by their achievements, service, and eminence have brought notable credit to the University.

Your meritorious accomplishments have become widely known to many colleagues and I am pleased to inform you that the faculty at a recent meeting voted unanimously to bestow upon you the recognition of a 1980 Distinguished Alumnus Award. . . .

. . . We extend to you our sincere congratulations and best wishes for a happy day with us in Cincinnati on April 25.

Cordially yours,
Kirk C. Valanis
Dean

Dad was one of nine nominees who received the Distinguished Alumnus Award in 1980 for "meritorious achievement, recognized stature, and conspicuous success in the imaginative blending of engineering education with highly productive endeavors in industry, professional activities, and public service." Dean Valanis presented the awards to the recipients at a special luncheon at U.C.'s Faculty Club on Friday, April 25. J.T. and Ruth accompanied Dad to the function and reported that in his speech of acceptance,

Dad gave a beautiful and clear-cut witness to the grace of God in his own life and his engineering career in India. His testimony was so moving that when he finished, the audience gave him a standing ovation. He was the first missionary that this secular university had honored in this way.

Dad was overjoyed when he discovered that one of the award recipients was a gentleman from India, Mr. Darbari Seth (M.D. in Chemical Engineering, class of 1956), who held several top managerial positions in Tata Enterprises, the largest agglomerate of industries in the private sector of India. He was the first foreign-born recipient in the history of the awards to receive the Distinguished Alumnus Award from the U.C. College of Engineering. Dad and Mr. Darbari Seth developed a meaningful friendship over the next four years. They corresponded regularly with each other, and whenever Dad returned to India he visited Mr. Seth in his home in Bombay. When Dad was hospitalized in Vellore, South India, for twenty-five days before his death, Mr. Seth, on several occasions, sent a special representative from his company in Madras (ninety miles from Vellore) with a beautiful bouquet of flowers and a card of sympathy.

Another source of honor for Dad was his high school *alma mater* in Tucson, Arizona. In June, 1980, he attended the commencement exercises of Tucson High School, in order to celebrate the 70th anniversary of his graduation. At that time he was the only living member of the class of 1910 which was the first graduating class of the newly organized Tucson High School. Dad was given special recognition at the commencement, and was asked to give the opening prayer and benediction. He distributed to each of the 375 graduates an attractive brochure with pictures and brief biographical sketches of the ten charter members of T.H.S., followed by a more detailed account of his own life story— boyhood days in Tucson, conversion and call, and missionary career in India. He challenged all the new graduates to seek God's plan for their lives.

For the next two years Dad was a familiar personage at the

commencement exercises of Tucson High School. Each time he had a part on the program and distributed a newly printed "commencement love letter" to each of the graduates.

At the 1982 commencement, Dad was given a red cap and gown to wear, and was asked to march in procession with all the graduates. Imagine his surprise, when the diplomas were being distributed, Principal Gilbert Carrillo called him forward, gave a beautiful public tribute to his life and career, and then announced to the audience of several thousand, "Arnett Seamands, it is the decision of the school authorities to include you as one of the 1982 graduates." And he handed Dad a diploma. Dad later remarked: "Wow, was I startled! I had graduated the second time from my beloved High School. Now I was ready for college at age 90. All the colleges wanted me as a student!"

On account of recent surgery, Dad was unable to be present at the 1983 Tucson High School Commencement, but in October of that year he was called to Tucson as one of five inductees into the Tucson High School Badger Foundation Hall of Fame, which began the previous year to "honor past students and employees of the High School for their accomplishments and service to the community, state and nation." The citation presented by President John L. Barringer, Sr., read as follows:

Dear Reverend Seamands

Congratulations on your induction to the Tucson High Badger Foundation Hall of Fame.

The Foundation today honors itself, the thousands of alumni, students, and all who have loved and nurtured Tucson High School throughout its illustrous history by recognizing you in this manner.

This is the highest tribute the Foundation can bestow.

At this point in time the Foundation has no certificate of award or merit, or momento of any sort which can be presented attesting to Hall of Fame membership.

With full awareness of the dedication and commitment to humane service which has basically characterized your lifestyle, it is our hope that this letter will serve as an identifying device attesting to your HALL OF FAME membership until such time as a more appropriate procedure is forthcoming.

Cordially and Sincerely,
John L. Barringer, Sr., President

On May 18, 1983, Dad received a letter from Harold Rogers, Kentucky member of the House of Representatives of the Congress of the United States. Mr. Rogers wrote:

Dear Dr. Seamands:

I recently came across the story of your life and your work as a missionary to thousands of people in the nation of India.

I was so impressed with your commitment to your work, and many years of service to your church and to humanity, that I included some remarks about you in the Congressional Record of this week.

Enclosed, please find a personal copy of the Record for that day, which includes on page E2304 the comments I made before the House of Representatives.

You are truly an inspiration, not only as a religious and humanitarian leader, but as a senior citizen who continues to be active for his life's pursuit. You are to be commended for your outstanding service to thousands, and those of us your junior should take note of your continuing efforts with an eye toward our own lives.

I wish you well, and hope that you will have many other trips back to India to preach, to teach and to help those less fortunate. If there is ever anything I can do to assist you in any way, please let me know.

With every best wish,

Sincerely,
Hal Rogers
Member of Congress

The tribute which appeared in the Congressional Record for May 17, 1983, read as follows:

A TRIBUTE TO DR. E. A. SEAMANDS

Hon. Harold Rogers
of Kentucky
in the House of Representatives
Tuesday, May 17, 1983

MR. ROGERS.   Mr. Speaker, there are few of us who are fortunate enough to enjoy the fruits of life until 91. Yet in my district, there is someone who can not only make that statement, but can still, even at that ripe old age, have a positive influence on the lives of thousands of people.

I am speaking of Dr. E. A. Seamands of Wilmore, KY, who just returned a few weeks ago from his latest missionary work in India. Dr. Seamands spent many years in India with his wife, Yvonne, before retiring in 1958. But every year since then, with a single exception, Dr. Seamands has made his way back to India to work with the peasants there whose lives he has touched.

While in India, Dr. Seamands would preach and minister, but he also worked with local communities, and would return to the United States each year with applications for assistance in building new churches and schools. In fact, Dr. Seamands has built more churches since his retirement, than he did during his entire career as a full-time missionary.

This past year, Dr. Seamands took part in the Dharur Jungle Jathra, a massive camp meeting. In 1923, when Dr. Seamands first organized the gathering, only 175 Indians attended. This time, a crowd of 80,000 was on hand. This speaks not only of Dr. Seamands' hard work, but of the profound impact he has as a religious leader in a land far away.

Mr. Speaker, I commend the attention of the House to Dr. E. A. Seamands, and ask you to join me in congratulating him for his outstanding service to humanity, and wishing him well as he continues his ministry in the future.

At the Dharur Jathra in November, 1983, the Chairman of the Bible Society of India presented Dad with a gold medal, symbolizing the John Hands Memorial Award of 1983, in recognition of his outstanding contribution in evangelism in the Church of India.

Though Dad was worthy of the many and varied honors that he received, he never allowed these awards to make him proud or puffed up. He always gave tribute to the grace of God in his life, and laid all these awards at the Master's feet.

THATHA'S LAST
FAMILY REUNION

Put all the leaves in the kitchen table, Mom.
For months you've been planning this special occasion.
From points north, south, and west they're coming home.
The house is all ready for the family invasion.

Two trips to the airport, a car rolling in,
Sisters' first gazes at each others' new babies.
Where's my room? and, What's for supper? and oh, what a din!
Break out the cookies, the apple pie, did you make me jilebes?

Anagrams and Scrabble — who made the best spelling?
Tennis duels, jogs through town, see an old friend.
Daddy's jokes — still funny after the hundredth telling.
Private talks, snacks around the clock. How quickly the days end!

Sunday dawns hot for the great all-clan picnic.
Aunts, uncles, kids and Thatha gather on the lawn.
Squirm through family pictures, then eat 'till you're sick.
Whose is that one? How old are you now? My, how you've grown!

Gnarled, faltering hands pat a small, fuzzy head
As half-blind squint meets bright blue gaze.
The patriarch and newborn span our life thread—
Tapestry woven through all our days.

One evening remains now, each moment we cherish.
Dad holds a baby on each of his knees.
Mom smiles at us all — for what more could I wish?
Thatha's voice catches, Wouldn't Grandma be pleased!

Suitcases closing; Have you seen Baby's Bear?
Gather toys, curlers, games—scattered all over the place.
Hugs, kisses, goodbyes — a bittersweet affair.
One last (?) long, loving look into Thatha's kind face.

The table shrinks back to its original size.
The pantry lies bare, save for last summer's canning.
Tiny fingerprints on a window bring tears to Mom's eyes.
Maybe next year — she thinks, and 'midst laundry, starts planning.

— Brandilyn Collins
Daughter of J.T. and Ruth

9

THE FINAL YEARS

After Mother's death, Dad had no responsibilities to hold him at home, so once again he set his face toward India. On November 1, 1981, he headed for his adopted land on his 10th shuttle-service mission. His Parsee contractor friend, Mr. Homi Irani, personally paid all his travel expenses.

Dad had been away from India for the past eight years, so leaders of the Methodist Church and his host of friends were most anxious to see him once again. The beginning pages of this book describe his memorable reception at Dharur Jathra that year. When the village Christians heard that Thatha would be present at the camp, they poured in by the thousands—70,000 in all. Bishop Elia Peter and Bishop Kariappa Samuel of the South India and Hyderabad Conferences, together with all the district superintendents and pastors of the two conferences, were present for the meetings. Spiritual tides were high, and the Sunday offering came to Rupees 65,000.

He traveled all across South India Conference area, and everywhere Christians went out of their way to welcome him in royal style. In procession they met him with bands and garlands, and paid him public tribute both in word and in song. Perhaps the most unique feature of the welcome was that in many places, not only did they place flower garlands around his neck, but they also presented him with garlands made up of Rupee notes all sewn together. In all, the love gifts came to around Rupees 5,000. Dad was overwhelmed by all this and he remarked over and over again: "All these years I have been raising money for the Church and people of India, and now they are turning around and showering me with money!" As would be expected, he privately turned all these gifts back into his church building projects.

During his seven-week tour he received applications from fifty-one rural congregations for help on their church buildings. Raising funds toward these projects would be sufficient "homework" for the next ten months back in the States.

Everywhere Dad went, people were fascinated by his pacemaker, village people in particular. They had no word in their language for this strange instrument, so they referred to it as "Thatha's battery." Word soon spread throughout the villages—"Thatha is running on a battery at 90!" Whenever he left for his next appointment, the people bidding him farewell would wave their hands and cry out, "We are praying that your battery will keep on working so we will be able to see you again!"

In the fall of 1982 Dad was back in India for another three-month service mission. Upon his return in February, 1983, he appeared very weak from severe bladder problems. We took him to a urologist in Lexington, and within a few days he underwent surgery for prostate. It took several months for him to get back on his feet, but by fall he was talking about going back to India for another mission.

J.T. and David, and his granddaughter Dr. Sylvia Seamands did their best to dissuade him from going, but his mind was made up. "I feel fine," he insisted, "I'm sure I can make it. Besides, I have twenty-five church building projects under way, and I need to see how they are coming along." So at the age of 92 he set off on his 12th shuttle service mission to India. By this time he had witnessed the completion

of almost 175 church buildings and was determined to bring
the total to 200 before he "finally retired for good."

Dad was present for the 60th anniversary of the founding
of Dharur Jathra (November, 1983), and was overwhelmed to
see over 85,000 Methodist Christians gathered in the tent-
tabernacle, singing and praising the Lord for all His manifold
blessings. Attendance at Dharur had grown during those
sixty years from between 150-175 to a host of 85,000, to become the world's largest Christian camp meeting!

Homegoing
Narrated by J.T.

In January of this year (1984), I was in India, escorting a
group of Asbury Seminary students on a three-weeks study
tour. We went to Bidar for a day-and-overnight visit and met
Dad there. He was in good spirits, joined us in the grand
welcome procession, and accompanied us as we visited four
new church sites. He had been in the country at that time
for two-and-a-half months and had taken everything in good
stride. His health appeared fine.

A few days later when our group was in Bangalore, Dad
joined us there, but immediately I noticed that he looked
very pale and weak. He was suffering from a bad case of
dysentery. A doctor came and examined him and gave him
some medicine, and I personally waited on him for the next
three days and nights. But there was no sign of improvement.
So I phoned the Methodist hospital at Kolar, forty miles
away, and a doctor and nurse came in an ambulance and took
Dad to the hospital. I knew Dad would be in good hands and
among friends, for Kolar had been the scene of his early ministry for several years. He had even supervised the construction of several new additions to the mission hospital. All the
staff members knew him and loved him.

Just before the ambulance pulled out, I said to the doctor:
"Please help my father to get back on his feet, and then make
arrangements to send him by plane straight to Bombay, so I

can personally escort him home with my group, eight days from now."

When Dad heard this he blurted out, "No! I can't do that. I still have two more churches to dedicate in Gulbarga District."

I said, "Dad, forget about the churches. The Bishop will dedicate them."

He just smiled.

Little did I realize that would be the last time I would see Dad on this earth.

Just a couple of days before my group was to fly out of Bombay, I received a telegram from Dad, saying he was feeling better and had decided to stick to his original schedule of returning to the States on February 5th. So I came on home with my students on January 19th. I was encouraged about Dad's health.

About ten days later we had a telephone call from Bishop Elia Peter in India, informing us that Dad had developed a respiratory infection and kidney failure, and that they were moving him from Kolar to the famous Vellore Christian Hospital for intensive care. The bishop also suggested that one of the family members fly out to be with Dad and to make some important decisions. Since I had recently seen Dad in India, my brother, David, decided he would make the trip. This would probably be his last chance to see Dad and have closure with him.

David was able to get a new passport in two days and an India visa in one day—all in record time—and fly out to India on a Boeing 747 jet. Because of his heavy duties back home in the church and seminary, David was able to stay in Vellore only four days, from Thursday to the following Monday morning. But he was able to make, ahead of time, the needed decisions and arrangements for Dad's funeral and burial.

David found Dad in a very weakened condition, but he was able to have some wonderful moments of deep fellowship with him. I will leave it to David himself to describe some of these precious moments, in the final chapter.

Dad lingered for another two weeks—much of the time in a coma—but the much-prayed-for "battery" kept him alive. Then at 4:30 a.m. on the morning of February 25th, he quietly slipped away to be with his Lord whom he had loved and served so well. Dad had often said that he would be quite happy to die in India, the land of his calling. In fact, he said, "If I die in India, it will be a little closer to Heaven than the United States!" So his final wish had been granted.

It was indeed difficult for all our family members to be ten thousand miles away from the scene of Dad's death, unable to attend his funeral and pay our last respects to him. We had to depend on the Church in India to perform the last rites. But perhaps this was the way it was meant to be. India was Dad's home; he had given sixty-four years of his life in service there. He loved India, and India loved him. He really belonged to India and the Christians there. So they had him all to themselves for the last few hours. And they arose to the occasion magnificently!

Dad's body was taken from Vellore to Bangalore by ambulance, and the funeral was held in the Richmond Town Methodist Church, where he had served as pastor during his first year in India and then for several years later. All the district superintendents and leaders of the conference came for the service. All Methodist schools across the conference were closed for the day in honor of Dad. The church was packed, and the service went on for almost three hours, as one person after another arose to pay tribute to their beloved Thatha.

Bishop Elia Peter delivered the message. Many of those present were Dad's spiritual sons and daughters in the Gospel. Some had been converted under his preaching; others had received their call to Christian service under his ministry. Others he had united in wedlock, or had laid hands upon for ordination to the ministry. All poured out their hearts in gratitude to God, and expressed their great love for this saint of God who had so tremendously influenced their lives.

Dad's body was laid to rest in the Christian cemetery in Bangalore, close to the graves of some of the great pioneers of the Christian Church in India, including the well-known Bishop J. W. Robinson. Bishop Robinson had gone out to Kolar especially to welcome Dad and Mother upon their arrival there in 1919.

On the same day that the funeral was held in Bangalore, India, a memorial service for Dad was conducted in the Wilmore United Methodist Church in Kentucky. Tributes were given by my brother, David, and me. Steve Seamands, David's son; Rick Sheppard, husband of J.T.'s daughter, Sandy; and Keith Mostad, husband of David's daughter, Debbie; all three of them ordained ministers, took part in the service. Naturally, tears were shed, but to the family this was not a time of mourning but of celebration—the celebration of a life lived victoriously and faithfully to the glory of God and to the extension of His Kingdom!

10

TRIBUTES TO THATHA

Letters of sympathy for our family and praise for Thatha poured in from all over the world. We want to share excerpts from a few of them:

A.M. Bhaskar, Methodist Church, Belgaum: We remember Thatha for his great interest in education for which cause he built hostels for poor rural children and built schools to educate them. He also built churches in rural and urban areas, the structures of which were blended to suit our cultural heritage. Along with this he built parsonages in villages as well as cities to make the life of pastors comfortable.

Thata was an engineer by qualification and profession but he was a great promotor of medical work, for which he established rural primary health centers and big hospitals like Holston Hospital. Thatha took great interest to train pastors theologically and he had a keen sense to choose suitable candidates for the ministry who have measured up to his expectation in service.

152

He has planned for community halls to develop spiritual, cultural, social activities and also to bring harmony and self sufficiency within Christian community.

We find that words are most inadequate to express our appreciation and gratitude to Thatha for his self-sacrificing services in full measure.

Miss Eva Logue, Retired Missionary: So many precious memories of dear Thata. One outstanding incident was his walking from Yadgiri to Yellary, a distance of about 20 miles, carrying potatoes and coconut during the Razakar time when we were cut off from the outside. He arrived just as a group of Hindus stood in front of our old village home, threatening to burn the place because we were protecting some Muslim women. The new quarters were then under construction. Thatha said, "If they are hiding anyone they will be in the new building." He led the mob away to search the new building and we sent the Muslim families on their way to the station to catch the train to another place. Thatha always arrived just when we needed him most. He was our spiritual father and we praise the Lord for him. Ajji (Mother) was a wonderful help to us also.

Mr. Luke from Yellari, who now lives in Zambia: Seeing Thatha Seamands through the eyes of an Indian lad like me, I can say that Thatha was a great man who served his fellow humans so well for more than half a century. He has left behind him not only J.T. and David to mourn his loss, but many souls he won for Christ. He was a great architect and builder of churches and souls. I belong to the third generation to have seen him in action. The history of the Methodist Church in South India will never be complete without Thatha . . . his energies were never exhausted nor his zeal for Christ.

Dr. Glenn R. Woodson, Pastor, Winnett, Montana: Earl was one of the many great models I had at Asbury. I'll always be grateful for his life and his influence on my life. I very much look forward to a reunion with him in Heaven. I'll probably have to stand in line to talk with him, though, considering how many thousands of people his life has touched.

Dr. M.D. Patterson, Larned, Kansas: Mrs. Patterson and I were conducting an eye camp at Yadgiri [India]. Tata came to conduct a service at Yellari. We rode with him in a jeep and I can still remember (this was in 1963) the exuberant and loving reception the Yellari Christian community gave him. We have a picture of him with his pith helmet smiling under the "Wel-come" sign as they exploded fireworks for him. . . . We have corresponded regularly over the years and we had the privilege of contributing to his air fare for, what proved to be, his final trip.

Mr. D. Samuel, Lay Leader, Hutti Methodist Church (India): On Saturday the 24th of March, 1984, the United Methodist Church, Hutti, conducted Memorial Service of Thatha, Dr. E. A. Seamands. In the same day afternoon, nearly 400 poor people were given lunch in memory of Thatha Seamands.

Mr. Charles Mark, Princeton, NJ: My immediate reaction was one of deep shock but mingled with joy for the fact that he breathed his last breath in India—the land of his adoption. Thatha belonged to that strange human species called the "missionary" which I doubt if we or our children would ever again come across such strange beings in their lives. And Lo and behold! Thatha was one of the finest spirits to tread the land of India. . . . Though I belong to the third generation of his first fruits, I believe that our generation is equally indebted to him as much as his first converts. . . . If you want to know South India Conference, study Thatha Seamands. In him there is nothing negative—everything positive.

Mr. E.S. Modak, Inspector General of Police, Bombay State (Retired): Thatha was, what the Bhagavad Gita would have called, a Stitapradnya, which means "a fully realised Soul." I think his secret was his childlike faith and simplicity, and as it has been written, of such is the Kingdom of Heaven. His heart was in India, and he must have been happy that he died here.

Dr. Raleigh Pickard, Missionary, Bidar, India: Thata's coffin was beautiful teak wood; he was dressed nicely and placed in the white, linen-lined casket along with his walking stick! When we get to heaven . . . we're gonna walk all over God's Heaven! I can truly say the funeral was not mourning and crying. Everyone seemed to be relaxed and inwardly joyful to be present and hear of the glorious life of Thatha. Only two missionaries were present—Dr. Hunter Mabry and myself. We were happy to stay in the background and witness the flood of love pouring from Indian hearts—many of which Thatha had won to Christ!

Dr. Gerry M. Mascarenhas, Dean, St. John's Medical College, Bangalore, India: While attending the funeral service of your dear father, memories of the past kept crowding my mind, as tribute after tribute was paid to this great man. Miss Sundaramma referred to him as a Saint, and a Saint he truly was. The service was beautiful. Both Marie and I cannot forget your dear parents. They were foster parents to us indeed when we were in Gulbarga 30 years ago, and I also recall the love and affection they showered on us when we were in Lexington 20 years ago.

Dr. Charles Gideon, Tucson, Arizona (formerly of India): Spiritually Thatha is with us always. He is our Saint! He brought joy to us, hope and comfort to us. When he stayed with us he gave us Christian *goodies* and left us some Christian *gordies* (songs of praises, Christian experiences and fellowship and Love). We adopted him as the head of our home. He listened to our family problems, and prayed and comforted us. We miss him a lot. We love him dearly.

Rev. Al Schneck, Retired Missionary: When we arrived in Bombay in 1949, there was Thatha to meet us and help us get started right. He carried baby Kathy on his shoulders while we shopped for "topees" and other things he considered essential to our well-being. Along the train route to Bangalore, he arranged for welcome parties and food. Mrs. Seamands brought us fried chicken and fresh coconut cake in Gulbarga—with cloth "serviettes!" And so it was through the years—he was always caring and very kind.

Miss V. Bhasker, Principal, Vanita Vidalaya High School, Belgaum: India has lost a saint and a builder. All educational institutions were closed on 27th February, 1984 in honor of Thatha. We share your grief and the greatest loss.

Rev. H. Samuel, Assistant Pastor, Bidar: In 1964 Thatha Seamands, after preaching on the subject "Harvest is plenty but labourers are few" gave an altar call to those who would join the ministry. A small group of young boys went forward. Thatha prayed with us. I was there among those, and today I am in the ministry because of him. His life and service has inspired me all these years. I visited him in Vellore Hospital. Though his voice was feeble, he said, "Jai Krist— I love you, and Jesus, I love you." He was a great missionary because of his love and sacrifice to us. He even lives in our hearts to inspire us to do God's will. He was faithful unto death.

Dr. Deena Sonna, Deccan, India: I will always remember Thatha establishing us in the work of the Lord in the villages of Deccan; he was like a father to us. He cared for our physical needs, and in times of trouble he was like an angel of mercy. The whole of the Deccan area will always remember him in gratitude.

Mr. Homi Irani, Architect and Builder—a special friend of Thatha's: Although there is deep sorrow it is mixed with gratitude to the Almighty for having spared Thatha and giving him the satisfaction of completing his life's work. He was like a father to me and his passing has left a big void. Somehow I had a premonition that this would be my Thatha's last meeting with us. Sitting in the good old rose-wood rocker of his [Thatha had made the rocker in the workshop in Kolar many years ago and had given it to Homi when he retired from service], I can still picture him enjoying the chilled Alphonso mango slices and cream and retracing all the old memories with Ajji (Mother). When I didn't feel I could build his social hall, Thatha became silent, then he called me over, took both my hands in his hands and said, "But Homi, this is named after *Yvonne* and you must build this for Ajji and me." I accepted with tears in my eyes, and I shall build a most beautiful hall for my Thatha and Ajji.

Miss Hira Dhanawadi, Raichur, India: Thatha loved us Indians, children and churches more than his own children. We used to wait for his coming to our places of service. All our school and hostel children loved him most. He had great concern for each one of us, especially for gypsy children. God has kept him here in our conference so that we will turn to God by Thatha's life and his selfless service and sacrifice.

Mrs. Helen Brown, New Jersey: So sorry such a nice person as Mr. Seamands had to die—he should have lived forever and the world would have been a better place to live. I respected him more than anyone I ever knew. He will be surely missed by a lot of people. There are so many happy memories.

Rev. Conrad P. Heins, Retired Missionary: We rejoice in the thought of what a glad and blessed welcome he has received from the Yesu Swami (Lord Jesus) that he loved and served so long. He warmed our hearts from the start when he first welcomed us to India and to the South India Conference, on the station platform at Madras in November of 1935. I will never forget the tour of Yadgiri District on which he took Hendrix Townsley and me back in 1938. It was mostly by bullock cart and on foot, but it was an exciting and enjoyable introduction to rural India and to village Christians! It included a thrilling three days at the Tintini Jathra. Mardy and I are glad that we had that final visit with our friend Arnett last year there at Wilmore. We were lifted by his vision of what the Church in India could be—and by God's grace would sometime be.

Mrs. Jo Kriz Fisher, Retired Missionary: Thank you for letting me know of the Triumphant Entry of Thatha! It couldn't have happened in a better place—among the multitudes whom he has led to the Lord, in a land where they might never have known Him had Thatha not given of himself—literally his life in joyful ministry. So long as I live, I will never forget his radiant personality!

Dr. Jim Fowler, International President of the Lions Club: To Mr. Billy C. Bradshaw, Secretary of Wilmore Lions Club. Dear Lion Bradshaw: It was with much regret that my wife, Aggie, and I learned of the death of Rev. E.A. Seamands. We wish to convey to you and your fellow Lions our condolences, and those of the International Officers and Directors. Please extend our heartfelt sympathies to his family.

His dedication to community service, compassion for the less fortunate, and love for family and friends will be remembered by all who knew him. While his death is a loss for your Club and your community, his life should encourage all of us to rededicate ourselves to the principles of Lionism and to even greater efforts in caring for others.

Lion Seamands, along with all Lions who pass away this year, will be remembered in a solemn ceremony at the International Convention.

A Tribute from J.T.
(Excerpts from his tribute given at the Memorial Service on February 27, 1984, Wilmore, Kentucky)

The life of my Father, Earl Arnett Seamands, is a marvelous illustration of the two aspects of the Christian life: the divine initiative and the human response.

His boyhood days in Tucson, Arizona, with its hot climate, dusty roads, and rugged frontier atmosphere, all were a preparation for life and work in tropical India. His tramping mile after mile in the mountains surrounding Tucson put him in shape for long hikes into the villages of India. His training as an engineer in the University of Cincinnati, drawing blueprints and building railway lines and bridges, all equipped him to become God's builder/engineer in the Methodist Church of South India. His conversion and call at Sychar Camp meeting gave him the inspiration to inaugurate the camp meeting movement in South India. After his conversion, his work among the drunks, prostitutes and down-and-out on the streets of Cincinnati, prepared him for service among socially despised, poverty-stricken Outcaste people of India. God had a job to be done in India and he needed a man to complete that job, so he was preparing Earl Arnett Seamands for the task ahead.

Dad's response to the divine initiative was wholehearted and complete. He was fully surrendered to the Lord and His will; no questions, no reservations, no regrets. He was one hundred percent for Jesus. "If you're going to be a Christian," he said, "be a Christian to your fingertips." As a result of this complete dedication to the Lord and his missionary calling, the fruit of the Spirit was evident in abundance in his life.

There was first of all the fruit of holiness. Dad was a real saint; he had a passion for Christ-likeness. His was not a legalistic, dogmatic, inflexible brand of holiness. The holiness he exhibited was so wholesome and winsome, and so practical. I can believe in the possibility of full salvation and a sanctified life, if for no other reason than that Dad demonstrated it in his own daily living. He was not perfect in every regard; he had his failures. He often aggravated us with his slowness and untidiness of his office. At times he irked us, when we had guests for dinner and he would ramble on and on about India. Yet his heart was right; his motive was pure.

Then there was the fruit of love in his life. He loved his Lord with all his heart, soul, mind, and strength. One of his favorite hymns was, "Oh, How I Love Jesus." He loved his family, all the way from his wife and sons down to every grandchild and great grandchild. If any member went astray, he agonized in prayer for his or her restoration. When Mother was bedridden for three-and-a-half years in Mayfair manor in Lexington, Dad hardly missed a day making the trip into the city to sit by her side, sing hymns and love songs, and pray with her. He made 1,116 trips to Lexington, a distance of about one-and-one-half times around the earth. A few years ago he wrote a letter to two of his granddaughters in which he said, "My darlings, I suddenly awoke to the fact that I have spent much money and time going to India to tell the people about Jesus, but I have neglected my own family. So I'm going to take the time and money to come to see you for a few days, and just sit down with you and talk to you about Jesus." And he did!

Most of all was his love for India and the Indian people. This was one of the great miracles of his life. The land he once despised in his youth became his homeland. The people whom he once described as "the scum of the earth" became his very own brothers and sisters, sons and daughters. He attributed this to the "baptism of love" that he received when he was filled with the Spirit on Clifton Avenue in Cincinnati.

I clearly remember when Dad and Mother were home in the States on their first furlough. I was just nine years of age. One day we heard a strange sound coming from the attic, so we went to investigate. Here was Dad beating on a large, round Indian drum. "Dad, what in the world are you doing?" we asked. He replied, "Oh, I just got so homesick for India I wanted to hear something that reminded me of India." Many times I heard him hold some villagers of India spell-bound, as he said to them in all earnestness: "For me to stay at home in my comfortable bungalow is like a *seramane* (prison), but to come among you dear people and spend time with you is like an *aramane* (palace)." In something close to disbelief they would click their teeth and nod their heads. Dad loved India so much that when he left for India the last time, he said, "If I take sick and die in India, don't worry, it will just be a short-cut to Heaven."

Another fruit of the Spirit evident in Dad's life was the joy of the Lord. Dad was always in good spirits; he was a happy Christian. It was a real treat just to be with him. Whenever he walked into a group of people, he seemed to lift the whole level of feeling; his radiance was catching. Through his influence, all the rural Christians of the Deccan area in south-central India dropped their usual form of greeting, *"namaskara"* (I bow my head to you). They said, instead, *"Jai Krist!"* (victory to Jesus). Dad didn't have much of a singing voice—mother was the musician in the family—but he loved to sing. Since mother's death, for the last two years, Dad has been living in our basement apartment, and often we could hear him singing as he came upstairs or worked at his desk. "It is Joy Unspeakable and Full of Glory" was his favorite chorus. In prayer meeting or even the regular worship service he often led out in a hymn or chorus.

One magnificent obsession captured Dad's heart and mind, and determined the priority of his life and ministry—that was his desire to introduce Christ to every person he met. He was not an eloquent preacher—he had no training in Bible or theology—but he was an effective witness for Christ. He witnessed to young and old, high and low, strangers and family members alike. When he received the Distinguished Alumnus Award from the University of Cincinnati in 1980, he gave his witness to the august group gathered there, and when he finished, the audience gave him a standing ovation. Whenever he was hospitalized, he spoke to the doctors and nurses about the Great Physician.

Some years ago, when the hippie movement was in full swing, a young hippie visited Asbury Theological Seminary during the Ministers' Conference. Several tried their hand at witnessing to the hippie. Some really "told him off . . ." After all, didn't he know better than to come into our sacred confines looking that way! Then one noon he was in the seminary cafeteria and Dad sat down opposite him. Dad said to the hippie, "We've been so glad to have you here this week. What's your name?"

And the hippie answered, "Steve."

"Steve! Why that's wonderful. I've got a grandson by the name of Steve, and I tell you, there's a great big place in my heart for anyone that's named Steve."

And so they talked on, and Dad asked him to tell him what it meant to be a hippie. Dad listened, made a few comments and finally said, "Well, that's funny, but I guess I'm just a happy, hippie Christian." And from there on Dad told Steve about God and His love—the truest, most wonderful kind of love!

When the meal was over, the hippie got up, crossed over to the other side of the table, put his arms around Dad and hugged him. When he sat down again with tears in his eyes, he said to the students seated next to him, "Man, that's real love!"

In November, 1982, when Dad went back to India on his 11th shuttle service mission, he was deeply concerned about the apparent lessening of evangelistic fervor in South India Conference. So he purchased a rarely-used Indian instrument called the *ektar* (one string), which consists of a small gourd with a round, wooden pole stuck through it, a small bridge, and one string. It plays only one note. Wherever he went he strummed the *ektar*, sang the chorus, "I Will Make You Fishers of Men," and then said to the church leaders and lay people, "The Church has only one string to play on, the string of evangelism. We must get back to the primary mission of the Church, that of proclaiming the Gospel and winning people to Jesus Christ."

We certainly miss Dad and his radiant presence, but we rejoice in his glorious home-going and coronation before the throne of the Chief Engineer of the Universe. In the words of Dr. E. Stanley Jones, "We Christians do not *deny* the *reality* of death, but we certainly can *defy* the *finality* of death."

They say that Earl Arnett Seamands is dead. Don't you believe a word of it! He has never been more alive than he is at this moment! *Jai Krist!* Victory to Christ!

A Tribute from David
(Given at the Memorial Service
on February 27, 1984, Wilmore, Kentucky)

J.T. has made the chief, formal tribute to Dad and his work in India. I want to share along a little more personal line. In my recent trip to visit Dad, I brought back only a few things. I gave away his clothing, except for one suit, an outfit in which he could be buried, some blankets and other things that he had. I brought back some blueprints for churches, records of gifts received and allocated on projects, undeveloped film of pictures he had taken, some gold rings and gifts that he had received. And then a couple of old, very worn books that I had never looked into before; I just threw them in the suitcase. A tiny pocket New Testament that he always carried wherever he went—I'd seen it many times. But another I had never seen: a very battered, tattered, torn, ancient devotional book. It's a well-worn copy of *The Daily Light*. You know what *The Daily Light* is. It is a compilation of Scriptures. It has a reading for every day of the year, a morning and an evening. Different Scriptures on different themes. I've been going through this ever since, and I feel like I've been quarrying in a secret gold mine.

This is a most remarkable document. This is not his daily journal—he kept a daily journal almost from the time of his conversion: one every year. There's a stack of them. This is his devotional book. It is the secret of his life. I don't know how to describe this thing . . . it is a journal, it is a daily diary, it is a weather report (I can tell you how many inches of snow we had on February 16, 1976, if you're interested), it's a hymnal. There are over 160 different places where it says, "Sing," and there's a song (the songs we have chosen for this Memorial Service have been chosen from it). "Down From His Glory," which Lynn Smith just sang, wins hands down. That's the most. "In Times Like These," which Bill Goold is going to sing, is a second. "It Is Joy Unspeakable and Full of Glory" is a close third.

This book is a hymnal, a songbook, it's a commentary on Scripture, it's a joke book, it's a sketchy autobiography, it's a family genealogical record. You have to be bilingual to read this; it's in English and in Kanarese. You've got to know both.

When I was younger I often wondered about my Dad's devotional life. I don't remember Dad having this strict, regular devotional life that is such a heavy on all of us in Wilmore. And that bothered me. He's supposed to be so wonderful. Where is this regular prayer life? This book has helped answer the question. Karl Barth used to lecture to ministers and say that when they got up their sermons, they should have one eye on the newspaper and the other eye on the Bible. And this book, which is at the heart of Dad's life, does exactly that. It is a heavenly book, but it is totally earthly. It is divinely vertical—yet utterly, humanly horizontal. It is an incarnate kind of Christianity—the Word becomes flesh. It's a God's eye view of life, but the eyes are completely human. It takes in all of life: life is lived to the full, it's lived abundantly, joyously. Everything in life, the most nitty-gritty daily events, are run through the strainer and filter of Scripture. All of life is evaluated in the light of walking with God. What has come to me in reading this in the last week, saturating myself in it, is one verse: "And Enoch walked with God." Dad simply lived and walked and talked with God all the time.

I now know why he talked so much about a book that influenced him greatly from the time of his early conversion. It is the classic book by Brother Lawrence, *The Practice of the Presence of God.* He was always quoting that book, and especially that passage in which Brother Lawrence said that he felt just as close to God when he was peeling potatoes in the kitchen as when he was taking Holy Communion.

This *Daily Light* is Dad's version of the "practice of the presence of God." It is a devotional book, but not in the sense of devotions that alternate between *reading* the Bible or *praying*, and then *living* over here in another compartment.

Rather than alternating, it is simultaneous; it doesn't alternate, it integrates. And he just lives all of life as an open dialogue with God, in a kind of continuous orientation with God. Now remember, this is not his daily journal, that's different. This is his devotional book, so that everything written had to be written on the side margins. Let me share just a few of his notations.

January 7th. That was the anniversary of his infilling of the Spirit. I don't know how far back this book goes, but a long way. "1915: my personal pentecost on Clifton Avenue in front of the University of Cincinnati. Then in Kanarese: *"Jaya Krist! Paramananda!"* That big word means "Heavenly joy." "Jaya Krist" means "Victory to Jesus."

February 3rd. "We moved into 400 Kenyon Avenue, 1958!!!"

1971. "Sing, 'Work for the Night is Coming.'" Underneath that, "I will, Jesus, signed, Thatha." *1979,* signed; signed again in *1980,* and again in *1981.* The Scripture readings are, "Be strong and work for I am with you, saith the Lord of Hosts." A big Kanarese *"Jaya Krist!"* under all of that.

April 6th. "Arrived in New York by air, 1957, [from India] for active retirement." *1980,* "Easter Sunday." *1983,* "I enter Good Sam Hospital. Sing, 'There's Something About that Name.'"

April 7th. "My prostate surgery, 1983." In Kanarese, *"Stotra"* – that means "praise." (Most people anticipating an operation don't say, "Jaya Krist, Paramananda, Hallelujah.") "Good Sam, room number 616." The reading for this day is, "As sorrowful, yet always rejoicing, as poor, yet making many rich, as having nothing, yet possessing all things." And other Scriptures in a similar vein. Dad's comment: "Howard Hughes died 1976, admitting, 'I'm not happy.'" Dad had taken the Scripture and has an arrow pointing to "Howard Hughes." His comment, "Possessing all things but having nothing." And then a Kanarese phrase, *"Ayyo!"* which means, "Alas!" It is a term of mourning.

April 15th. (Remember this is his devotional book.) Right on the top margin he wrote "Income Taxes. Sing, 'In the Name of the Lord We Have the Victory.'" On the same date in *1981,* he wrote, "Linda and Mark arrive," and he has added some more Scriptures.

April 15th for the evening reading. "Seekest thou great things for thyself? Seek them not." The whole reading is on that subject. What's the comment? *1977:* "Pete Rose and Don Gullett." Do you remember when they were trying to get millions of dollars for their contract? "Seekest thou great things? Seek them not." Comment, "Pete Rose."

May Day, May 1st, 1978: "My pacemaker decision." When he first decided to have it. There are many others for May 1st. *1979, Tuesday,* "Day of Prayer in Washington, D.C." *1983.* "The end of Ichthus. The Lord is here." Many references to Ichthus.

May 10, 1978. "I enter Central Baptist Hospital, Lexington for my pacemaker. Room 488. Lunch: meat, mashed potatoes, broccoli. Supper: chicken noodle, small ham." Here are the names of the nurses, where they come from, their problems. One of those nurses later said to us, "I never met a man like this before in all my life." He was interested in their problems, always praying for them. Later, "Dr. Mayo visited," and so forth. Over here another menu.

8 a.m. Now, Dr. Mayo inserts the pacemaker. "A-Okay!" Amazingly enough, *May 12th,* all the Scriptures are about the heart. "The love of God is shed abroad in our hearts by the Holy Spirit given to us." And so forth. Dad's comment: "Blessed are the *Pace*makers. . ." Wait until you hear the rest of the Scripture now. "Blessed are the *Pace*makers, for they bring God's strength and newness of life to the fainthearted. Amen!" And what's alongside that, besides all the religious comments? "Reds, 4; Phillies, 3!"

Pentecost Sunday, next day. "Cold, 40-46 degrees. Reds 4, Phillies, 7. *"Ayyo!"* he says.

May 29th. Three years later. "My 1,000th visit with Yvonne at Mayfair Manor. 36,000 miles. Let us labor to enter into that rest." Another year, same date, "I'm out of Good Sam Hospital."

July 10th is an interesting one, because this same Scripture appears several times. "My son, give me thine heart," and in every case, I don't know which is the real date, but in every case, he writes, "Tucson, AZ. Arnett, 1910. I rejected Christ." And I remember him telling about the time when God spoke to him way back in high school, "Son, give me your heart," and he didn't do it. That is recorded every time this Scripture is, and a date for Tucson, Arizona. And he also says, "Ayyo!" But there is also happiness on that day. "Jason Mark Seamands, born, 1974."

July 11th. "My darling Yvonne's birthday." And there follows year after year the celebrations; finally, she's in the rest home. "Happy party in Mayfair Manor, 3 p.m. Cake, ice cream." *1982.* "She is not here." She had died. The Scripture he has underlined there with an arrow pointing from "She is not here" — "We have not a high priest which cannot be touched with the feelings of our infirmities." And he has written above that, "Indeed!"

I could go on. I think you get the point. Again and again these marvelous correlations between life and devotion in a most amazing way.

Finally the last one. *1983,* "Fly with George Garden to India, Mission Number 12." Then, "In the air to India, 1983." He's reading it on the airplane. "Blessed is the man that heareth me, watching daily at my gates, waiting at the posts of my doors." And it is all about service.

There's also history in this *Daily Light* copy.

October 6, 1973. "Israel, war with Egypt."

We get near the end. J.T., I think he hurt himself more than we realized there in Bangalore. It was the beginning of the end.

November 8th, 1983. "Bed time, I fell in the bathroom of BGHS (Baldwin Girl's High School). Hurt my back severely." Next day, *Wednesday,* "In bed." Next day, "In bed." Next day, "In bed." But on Sunday he preaches in the old Richmond Town Methodist Church, where they probably are having his great funeral just about now.

The great Quaker saint, Thomas Kelly, says that "there is a deeper level of prayer. It is the secret of a deeper devotion, a more subterranean sanctuary of the soul, where the light never fades, but burns a perpetual flame, where the wells of living water rise up continuously, day by day, and hour by hour, so that we are perpetually in worship while we are very busy in the world of daily affairs" (*A Testament of Devotion*).

Thatha walked with God. It was a natural, joyous, guilt-free walk. It was hard to tell the difference between the sacred and the secular in his life because it was all a continuous dialogue with the Lord. Two times stand out more than any others as illustrations of this natural dialogue with God. I was seven years old in Kolar, India. The news of the Great Depression came to us—the 1929 crash. We got a letter from the Andrew Mellon Bank in Pittsburgh, Pennsylvania, that all our life savings were gone. The bank had closed. Mother cried hysterically; Dad talked with God.

The second was the day our son died. By the time the news that little David was ill reached Mother and Dad and they arrived at our mission station, it was late at night. We were on the back porch in Bidar. Mother said, "How's little David?" I said, "I'm sorry, Mother, but we buried him this morning at ten." There was a long silence. My Dad lifted his face and said, "Lord, I don't understand this." That was all. And then we walked into the bungalow together.

And so it was when I arrived at his bedside at Vellore Hospital a few days back. He couldn't understand that either. Not *my* coming, but why *he* was there. "I've so much to do, David," he said. "How did this happen to me? How is this possible? How did I get in this mess?" he said. "I've got all these churches to build." He wept. He was depressed because his work had been cut short at such an early age! So an inspired thought came to me; I know it came from the Lord. I said, "Dad, I want you to repeat a verse along with me. Repeat the words after me, will you do that?"

"Yes, David."

I said them slowly and he repeated them. "I have finished the work."

His voice was very low, I had to put my ear down to hear. "I have finished the work."

"Which Thou gavest me to do."

"Which Thou gavest me to do."

I said, "Say it again, Dad." "I have finished the work which Thou gavest me to do." We said it about five times. I asked, "Who said that?"

Dad answered, "Jesus."

I asked again, "After how many years did Jesus say that?" He replied softly, "Just three years."

I said, "Dad, I think *you* can say that after 92 years!"

He nodded his head and said, "Yes, I think I can. 'I've finished the work Thou gavest me to do.'" And then he sort of went into a coma. That was on Thursday.

On Sunday afternoon there was that final spurt of life which so often happens near the end. He was wide awake. His mind was like a steel trap. He was punning in Kanarese. He loved to do that. Memory was clear as a crystal. He talked about Camp Sychar. He talked about his conversion, his call. He talked a lot about Wesley Chapel in Cincinnati. A dear friend knocked at the door and brought the hospital choir into the room; they packed in, about 30 beautiful young Indians. They sang in four-part harmony a lovely arrangement of "Amazing Grace." Oh, how Dad wept and shouted the praises of God! The songs began to flow again, almost the last really clear thing that he did was sing. Of course, you know it had to be — "Joy Unspeakable and Full of Glory." And then he brightened up and said, "Oh, David, I've got it!"

"What have you got, Dad?"

He glowed. "I've got joy unspeakable and full of glory! Heavenly joy!"

And then he lapsed back. I can only think of Charles